C1 Vocabulary: 100 Exam Keywords for Advanced English

Albert Bowkett

ISBN:
9781522086642

CONTENTS

INTRODUCTION

One of the major challenges in moving from B2 (intermediate) to C1 (advanced) level English is the additional vocabulary requirement - approximately 600-1000 keywords*, many of which are more complicated in meaning and form.

Furthermore, in the C1 exam, candidates are expected to use this new vocabulary to **discuss more complex ideas**, and **construct arguments** in a more academic way.

(*Here, 'keyword' means a high-frequency or important word that is part of a 'word family' - for example, 'explain' is the keyword in a word family that includes: unexplained, explanation, explaining, explanatory)

Coursebooks and topical conversation practice will give you the basics of what you need to pass the C1 exam but many people find that this general preparation is **not enough**.

Many learners encounter a particular difficulty in the C1 exam: the special '**exam vocabulary**'. It's one of the reasons that even native speakers can also fail EFL exams like the IELTS, CAE, or TOEFL!*

(*A recent case reported in the media showed that some native-speaking Australian health workers were failing to gain the IELTS level required in order to work in the UK National Health Service. One of the main problems was academic essay language.)

This special 'C1 exam vocabulary' consists of:

- Technical or academic 'exam-speak' used in C1 exam tasks
- Special ways in which words may be used in the C1 exam
- 'Favourite' words, which EFL examiners want to see and hear

This book contains an essential selection of 100 of these exam keywords and phrases, which are routinely used in the IELTS, CAE, and TOEFL exams at C1 level.

Unlike other dictionaries or simple word lists, this book gives examples of **the special ways in which the words and phrases are typically used in the C1 exam/at C1 level**. Typical mistakes are also highlighted, and model answers are provided, together with any extra information learners might find useful.

The keywords in this book are divided into ten units, which are organised to reflect the special requirements of the C1 exam. Each keyword is presented in the same format:

(Keyword)
Example in an exam-style sentence:
What does it mean?
How to use in an exam-style answer:
Be careful! (common mistakes/extra information)

At the end of each unit, there is a 'test' exercise (with answers provided) for learners to practise using the words, and to check their understanding.

This book is intended as an additional study resource for students preparing for the C1 exam in English. Learners can study the units consecutively, working through the whole book step by step, or this book may be used as a quick reference guide, to check a certain word or topic as and when required.

UNIT 1: TASK WORDS AND ANALYSIS I

At C1 level, exam tasks are more complicated - if you don't respond in your answer to all the task requirements in the right way, you risk an automatic fail for that question or task. **This means it is crucial that you read the task/question very carefully.**

But what if the task/question includes technical language - 'exam-speak' - that isn't used in everyday English?

This unit highlights and explains ten essential 'exam speak' words which frequently cause problems for C1 exam candidates.

1. Aspects

Example:

These pictures show people travelling. What different **aspects** *of travel do the pictures show?*

What does it mean?

An aspect is a 'side', like one side of a mountain or one side of a house. In exam questions, 'aspect' has the figurative meaning: 'subtopic' or 'key feature'.

'Aspects of travel' means 'sides of travel' or 'subtopics of the topic: travel'.

So: if 'travel' is the main topic, what are the subtopics? Which subtopics do the pictures show? Examples of *subtopics of travel* are: holidays, business travel, delays, luxury travel, and so on.

How to answer:

The pictures show different **aspects** *of travel: picture one shows the daily hassle of getting to work, while picture two represents the luxury side of travel.*

Be careful!

This is a favourite question in the CAE speaking exam, part 2 (solo picture comparison).

Identifying aspects is NOT the same as describing what is happening in a picture or in a story. An aspect is always an abstract 'side' of a bigger topic. A picture might show people talking in a café. If the task requires you to identify aspects of 'spare time', then you should NOT say/write *''this picture shows two people talking in a café''*; you should say/write *''this picture shows the* **social aspect** *of spare time''*.

2. Contradict

Example:

*How does the second witness **contradict** the first speaker's account of the accident?*

What does it mean?

'*Contra*' means 'against/opposing', and '*dict-*' is related to speaking, so **to contradict** means to 'say against' or 'oppose'.

If you say the car was red and I say it was green, I am **contradicting** you.

This is not the same as giving a different opinion: If you say the film was great and I say it was terrible, this is just a different opinion, not a **contradiction**.

How to answer:

*The second witness says she clearly remembers the man stopping to tie his shoelace before standing up and crossing the road normally. This **contradicts** what the first person says about the man running onto the road.*

Be Careful!

Contradict (verb), **contradictory** (adjective), and **contradiction** (noun) may be used to describe not just speech but also books, articles, films, pictures, or in fact any kind of media which presents something as a 'fact' which is the opposite of another 'fact'.

A person can also contradict himself/herself, if he or she gives two different answers to the same question. In this case, that person's second statement can be called '**self-contradictory**'.

3. Convey

Example:

*Which word in the third paragraph of the story extract best **conveys** a strong sense of fear?*

What does it mean?

In exams, **convey** is often used to describe the way words, pictures, or music (or any media) 'deliver' or express a message or feeling, usually indirectly.

There is a difference between talking about fear directly, and **conveying** fear:

1. The people were visibly worried (directly talking about fear)
2. The minutes passed with agonising slowness (conveying fear indirectly)

How to answer:

*The word 'agonising' strongly **conveys** not just worry, but a real sense of fear that is compared to the agony of extreme physical pain.*

Be Careful!

The question 'Which word **best** conveys fear?' might ask you to find a more extreme synonym in the text (for example, 'terrified') or it might be a more indirect word like in the example answer above.

You have to use your judgement to decide which word **best** or **most** expresses the sense of fear. The C1 exam often requires you to choose the 'best right answer' from two or more 'right answers'.

4. Discuss

Example:

Some people think sport should be compulsory for all children at school, while others believe sports lessons should be optional.

Discuss *both sides and give your opinion.*

What it means:

'**Discuss**' has a particular functional meaning for academic essays and debates. It means you should talk about the topic in an <u>objective</u>, scientific way, identifying (or speculating about) the main issues and arguments 'for' and 'against', using <u>discursive</u> language to 'remove yourself' and your personal opinions from the argument (*most people who think this say that../ some people also argue that.../ it is often argued that.../ the counter to this argument is that...*, and so on). Unit 6 provides some vocabulary and advice for writing a discursive essay.

If the question ALSO asks you to give your opinion, you should add your opinion only <u>after</u> you have first identified the main, popular arguments 'for' and 'against', in an objective way.

How to answer:

The classic argument for full participation in sport at school is that 'if it was good for the Ancient Greeks, it must be good for us.' Sport has obvious benefits for health, and studies show that short periods of physical exercise can also help to improve children's concentration, memory, and behaviour in class. Supporters of sport in school also argue that sport teaches children important lessons in teamwork, strategy, and discipline.

On the other side of the argument are the 'pro-choice' supporters, who often complain that school sport is old-fashioned and time-consuming, and only of real benefit to a handful of talented young athletes. These parents argue that those children who are good at sport and enjoy these lessons should be given the option of extra sports training, while those children who are more suited to other subjects should be allowed to focus more on those.

Personally, I can sympathise with both sides of the argument and I believe a compromise is possible, with some short and simple sports classes organised for all children every day, and optional, more formal sports training provided for those who choose to take sport more seriously.

Be Careful!

1. This is a favourite essay question format in the IELTS exam. There are also variations:

'Discuss the advantages and disadvantages'
'Discuss the main issues involved'
'Discuss possible solutions to the problem'
'Discuss possible ways of tackling the problem'

In all of these variations, the word '**discuss**' has the same special academic meaning: you should be objective and examine more than one side to the topic or argument.

2. 'Discussion' and 'conversation' can mean the same thing (*we had a discussion/conversation/talk about revision topics*) but a 'discussion' may often be more specific, analytical, and formal, while a 'conversation' may often be rather general and informal.

5. Factors

Example:

Read the newspaper report. What were the main **factors** *which led to the closure of the factory?*

What does it mean?

Here, **factors** means *'influences'* or *'things which contributed to a particular effect'*, either directly or indirectly. In this particular example, it means, *'what were the main events and reasons which resulted in the factory closing?'*

How to answer:

According to the newspaper report, the main **factor** *behind the factory closure was poor strategic management at the top of the company - in particular a failed project in which too much money was spent on developing and marketing a new product. A second* **factor** *was the location of the factory far from main transport links, which made it harder to deliver goods on time. The final nail in the coffin was a failed health and safety test.*

Be Careful!

1. 'Factors' can also be used in a question about the future, for example:

'What **factors** *will need to be considered when planning an activity program for the exchange students?'*

Here, '**factors**' means - '*special things to think about*' that will affect the final plan.

2. **Factor** has other meanings:

- To **factor (sth) in** (phrasal verb: '*to include an extra consideration in a plan*' - '*We will need to* **factor in** *changing exchange rates when planning our holiday abroad next summer*'.
- '*To increase by a* **factor of** *10*' (noun, mathematical: to multiply/divide)
- '*X factor*' (noun, colloquial) a hard-to-describe 'magic ingredient' or special quality, especially in sports competitions, artistic performance, or product marketing.

3. '**Factor**' is not connected with 'factory'.

6. Infer

Example:

"What can we **infer** *from the statement 'companies will almost certainly want to review staffing levels in line with the more competitive market conditions'?"*

a. *Unemployment numbers will likely rise*
b. *Employment numbers will likely rise*
c. *Employment numbers will be unaffected*

What does it mean?

To infer means '*to guess*', '*to deduce*' or '*to draw a conclusion*', or even '*to read between the lines*' (fill in the gaps/recognise a suggested meaning). To infer means to guess at something that is suggested logically or indirectly by the information, even when we don't know all the details or outcomes for sure: *we may **infer** from the large library that the owner of the house is a keen reader.*

How to answer:

'The answer is (a) unemployment numbers will likely rise.'

(If market conditions are more competitive, it means companies will need to reduce costs, which will probably mean cutting jobs, which will in turn likely increase the number of people who are unemployed.)

Be Careful!

1. Native speakers often confuse the verbs '*imply*' and '*infer*' but in fact they are opposites.

    Imply means '*to suggest*'; Infer means '*to guess*':

    The statement implies that unemployment will rise.
    I inferred from the statement that unemployment will rise.

2. In exams, **infer** may often be used in the passive:

*What can **be inferred** from the statement? (What logical conclusion can you make from the statement?)*

7. Influence

Example:

*Describe a positive **influence** from your childhood.*

---

*How can surroundings **influence** our productivity?*

What does it mean?

In the first example, **influence** is a noun, with the meaning '*a power to change or affect someone or something*'. When we talk about *personal influences*, we mean what things or which people have affected your personal development, character, life choices, beliefs, and tastes.

In the second example, **influence** is a verb with the same meaning '*to affect*' or '*to change*'.

How to answer:

*I think growing up in the countryside had a positive **influence** on me. Many children complain of boredom in the countryside but I think it forced me to create my own activities and appreciate the detail in nature. My uncle was a biologist and he told me the names of all the plants and animals and explained how they all operated in a shared system.*

---

*Having the right surroundings is very important for productive work or study. Few people appreciate noise and distractions when they are trying to work. However, not everyone considers the more subtle **influences**, for example: sitting next to a window is proven to help you work better, both physically because daylight is good for your eyes, and mentally, because being able to look into the distance occasionally helps us to collect and focus our thoughts, and also has a calming effect. Colours are important too, with the power to affect our mood in different ways...*

Be Careful!

1. '**Influence**' doesn't mean '*a caused b*', but rather: '*a helped to push b in this direction*', or '*a helped to provide the conditions or the inspiration for b to happen*'. '*Bob Dylan's lyrical style was **influenced** by folk and blues singers, as well as classic literature.*'
2. **To be influential** means 'to have a continued important effect on someone or something,' for example: '*Viking mythology continued to*

*play an **influential** role in early English Literature long after Christianity had taken hold'; 'Although Sir Roderick keeps a low profile, he is said to be very **influential** behind the scenes.'*

8. Outweigh

Example:

Ten years ago, it was predicted that by today, at least a third of all workers would be working from home. Although 'home-office' has become more popular, less than one in ten people work in this way today.

*Do the disadvantages of 'home office' **outweigh** the advantages?*

What does it mean?

'Outweigh' is a verb that is only usually used in analysis (and exams!) It means *'weigh more than'*, or *'be greater than'*. In the above example, it means *'are the disadvantages greater than the advantages?'*

How to answer:

*The advantages of working from home are obvious: the time and expense saved from not having to commute daily to the office, the added flexibility regarding childcare, and a comfortable work environment. With the huge developments in IT communication over the last ten years, working from home has become more and more feasible for more companies and employees. There are however, notable disadvantages to 'home office': the distractions of home and family responsibilities like cleaning, visitors, and children is a major issue. Also, in practice, some workers find phone and internet is a poor substitute for key face to face meetings with colleagues and clients. Without a doubt, the pros are **outweighed** by the cons for some professionals. However, I suspect the main factors preventing more people from choosing home office are employer inflexibility and also poor quality internet connections.*

Be Careful!

This is a common question format in the IELTS exam, usually used with 'advantages and disadvantages'. You should describe at least one advantage and one disadvantage before saying which is greater.

9. Perspective

Example:

*Read the proposal and the notes taken from the public meeting. How successful do you think the shopping centre project will be, from the **perspectives** of (a) a local resident (b) a shop owner.*

What does it mean?

A **perspective** is a view of something - similar to an aspect but here we mean rather the viewer's position and the particular way he or she sees a subject from that position. The same mountain will appear differently viewed from an alternative **perspective**.

In the exam, **perspective** will probably be used figuratively to mean 'opinion', or 'one person's *view* of a topic or issue'. A **perspective** may be expressed as the *'point of view'* of a certain type of person (for example, **a young person's perspective**) or it may be more abstract (for example, **an emotional perspective, a scientific perspective**).

How to answer:

The shopping centre will probably be very popular with local residents, who like the idea that this dirty part of the city will be developed. However, residents aren't so happy with the current plans for parking, so this part of the plan will need improvement to ensure success. For shop-owners, the main concern is that shoppers will no longer visit the old centre, and the shop-owners see this as a long-term problem for their businesses and the life of the city.

Be Careful!

Don't confuse **perspective** with *prospective* or *prescriptive*!

Perspective means 'view' or 'opinion'
Prospective means 'future' or 'potential'
Prescriptive means 'instructive' or 'rule-based'. A prescription is an instruction, but it is also the word used for the drugs or remedy a doctor recommends to a patient.

10. To what extent

Example:

The government should take active steps to ensure people make healthier eating choices.

*To **what extent** do you agree or disagree?*

-----

*To **what extent** does advertising affect our choices?*

What does it mean?

To what extent is a formal way of saying *'how much: yes/no?'*

How much do you agree or disagree?
How much does advertising affect our choices?

How to answer:

I agree partly with the principle of government intervention regarding healthy eating. Specifically, I believe strongly that government has a responsibility to force food producers to maintain high standards and also to be clear and honest in labelling food products. I also think government needs to take the lead in preventing food producers from including high volumes of sugar in foods that are then aggressively marketed towards children.

However, there is a limit to how much government intervention is effective or appropriate. The main problem is that these laws and restrictions are a blunt instrument which can over-simplify the problem and anyway, food producers and retailers usually find clever ways to get around the rules. This is why I think that any government initiative needs to be met by personal responsibility - we all need to take personal steps to do what we know is sensible regarding our diets.

Advertising can affect our choices in obvious ways by making us more aware of one particular version of a product, or it can work in more subtle ways over a period of time to influence our ideas of things like success, fun, and beauty...

Be Careful!

1. **To what extent** means *'how much (yes or no)'*, NOT *'how much does it cost/how much water...'* and so on.

2. Do not confuse with '*to which extent*'. This is an unusual construction which has a different meaning (*which option*). It is unlikely you will need to use this construction.

UNIT 1 TEST!

Fill in the gaps using the ten keywords from this unit

1. The university professors were impressed by the young student's ability to confidently _____ serious topics and issues.

2. The new director's film is roughly edited and lacks polish but for me, the fresh, truly original style and perfect casting are enough to _____ any technical reservations.

3. For an alternative _____ on the plays of Shakespeare, it's worth reading this new guide, available to purchase in all good bookshops, or to download as an e-book.

4. Although the main cause of the crash was confirmed as poor lighting, tiredness and wet weather were also identified as _____.

5. Many people think nursing is just about checking blood pressure and cleaning beds but in fact there are many different _____ to this vital profession.

6. Now we are going to hear from a psychologist who is interested in how early childhood experiences can _____ a person's long-term attitude to saving - and spending - money.

7. I wanted to ask the boss for a pay rise but from the closed door and the frown on the secretary's face I was able to _____ that this was not a good moment.

8. This avant garde painting, left deliberately unfinished, is said to _____ the fleeting nature of the immediate present moment.

9. It isn't really my business, so I'm not sure _____ I should show sympathy or not.

10. The politician was widely mocked after she managed to _____ what she had said only a moment earlier about the controversial tax policy.

Answers: 1. *discuss* 2. *outweigh* 3. *perspective* 4. *factors* 5. *aspects* 6. *influence* 7. *infer* 8. *convey* 9. *to what extent* 10. *contradict*

Congratulations! You've completed 10% of your essential exam vocabulary revision for the C1 exam!

UNIT 2: TASK WORDS AND ANALYSIS II

1. According to

Example:

According to *the second student, what is the main problem with the university website?*

What does it mean?

According to means '*what one person or thing says or believes*'.

According to is used to show that a comment/opinion belongs to a certain person or thing and that the comment/opinion is not necessarily true, and that you don't necessarily agree with it.

According to is followed immediately in the sentence by the person or thing, and then their opinion or belief.

How to answer:

The second student complains that for him, the university website is useless because the coding is not compatible with his smartphone.

Be Careful!

1. This is a common question format in all C1 exams. Often, there will be more than one opinion in a text or recording. You must first find <u>the opinion which belongs to the person or thing mentioned in the question</u>. It might be the writer's opinion (*according to the writer*), it might be the interviewer's opinion (*according to the interviewer*), or it might be the general opinion expressed in one particular text (*according to the first article*).

2. If the person or article has more than one opinion, you must decide which is the strongest or most important opinion that best matches the question. For example:

> '*Question 1.* **According to** *Suzie, what was the most memorable part of the evening?*'

- You read the text/listen to the recording, and you identify these opinions:

Suzie's first opinion - *The food was tasty.*
Jill's opinion - *My food was awful.*
Suzie's second opinion - *The band was absolutely amazing - they brought the house down!*
Suzie's third opinion - *I liked the comedian too; she told some great jokes*
The radio host's opinion - *It was an unforgettable location in a beautiful castle by the sea.*

Which is the correct answer? First of all, the question begins '*according to Suzie*'. This means the answer cannot be Jill's opinion, or the radio host's opinion. Secondly, Suzie has three opinions - regarding the food, the band, and the comedian. Which is her most positive opinion?

'*Absolutely amazing*' is the strongest of Suzie's positive opinions, which means 'the band' was the most memorable part of the evening, **according to** Suzie.

2. Address *and* Tackle (a problem or issue)

Example:

*Write an email in reply to your friend. You should **address** his main concerns in an appropriate tone.*

----

*Supermarket trolleys are often taken from the store premises and then dumped - blocking roads, walkways, and rivers and causing an eyesore, as well as extra expense for the supermarkets and local council who must then recover them. Suggest ways of **tackling** the problem.*

What does it mean?

To address (something) means literally '*to formally speak to*' (*the speaker addressed the audience*). **Address** is also used sometimes to describe the consideration of a problem or challenge.

To tackle literally means '*to physically meet an opponent*', like in football or rugby. **To tackle a problem** means to take real action to solve a problem.

Address and **tackle** share a similar basic meaning and may sometimes be used in the same way to mean the same thing (responding to a problem). However, **addressing** a problem may be more about formal assessment and recommendation, while **tackling** a problem has the sense of more robust, practical action.

How to answer:

Hello Carl,

I understand your concerns about our new flatmate and you are right to raise them before we make a final decision about whether we should agree to him staying for a longer period.

I totally agree that Mike's loud music is a nuisance and also that he shouldn't smoke in the toilet, as this is a shared area. To give him the benefit of the doubt however, we haven't actually spoken to him about these complaints yet so maybe he doesn't realise he is bothering anyone.

Your third point about him bringing people back to the flat is perhaps a little unfair - you and I bring people back to the flat, too. As long as his guests are well-behaved I don't think we can have one rule for us and another for him. I think it's important to be consistent and fair.

Accordingly, I suggest that we call a house meeting and make all these things clear. Of course, if Mike then fails to follow the agreed rules then we will have to ask him to leave. Hopefully it won't come to that.

Best regards,

Greg

Regarding the problem of dumped supermarket trolleys, it would seem prudent to consider the various parties involved, namely: the owners of the stores, the local council, and the people who actually take the trolleys from the store and discard them once their immediate needs are met. All of these parties have a role to play in clamping down on and preventing this nuisance.

First of all, the owners of the stores should operate a coin-return system on their trolleys if they do not already do so, to encourage shoppers to return trolleys and collect their deposits. At the same time, the local council needs to use the street cameras they already control to make some prosecutions to deter other would-be offenders. Finally, the offenders themselves should be made to pick up litter - including dumped trolleys - as part of their punishment.

Be Careful!

This is a common question format in writing tasks. If you are asked to address certain points or to suggest ways of tackling certain problems - be sure to include ALL the points requested in the task instructions: If the task asks you to suggest ways of tackling litter, noise, and graffiti, and you suggest ways of tackling litter, noise, and stray dogs, **you will probably fail the writing task.**

It sounds simple, but a surprising number of students fail for this reason. When you are rushing in the exam, it's easy to miss something out, so be sure to check your answers, and for all writing tasks, be sure to include in your answer ALL of the required points (unless the task clearly says you should choose from the points).

3. Distinguished (from)

Example:

*In the article, how is the techno DJ **distinguished from** other types of musician?*

What does it mean?

Distinguished from means 'different from', but there is an extra grammatical feature: 'Distinguished' is a 'Verb-3' (past participle) <u>passive</u> adjective, so it suggests an active agent. See the two questions below:

> *In the article, how is the DJ **different from** other types of musician?*
> (This question asks for YOUR opinion/judgement, based on the text).

> *In the article, how is the DJ **distinguished from** other types of musician?*
> (This question asks you to explain how the WRITER distinguishes between the DJ and other musicians).

How to answer:

*The writer makes the interesting but provocative claim that the techno DJ is a 'composer-performer', like a modern Mozart playing all the instruments himself, while other musicians are simply performers. The writer uses this **distinction** to support the book's central claim that digital technology represents a 'third age' in Art history.*

Be Careful!

1. 'Distinguished' is a Verb-3 passive adjective but it doesn't *always* point to an active agent; in the sentence below, the active agent is simply 'people/anyone' - *people/anyone can distinguish the Kingfisher.*

*The kingfisher is easily **distinguished** from other birds by its distinctive blue and orange plumage.*

2. Used on its own, **distinguished** is a synonym for 'celebrated', 'successful', 'noble', or 'VIP':

*The charity opera always attracts a large number of well-known faces and **distinguished** guests.*

3. The direct synonym of 'different' is the simple adjective: **distinct**.

4. Emphasise

Example:

*What aspect of village life is **emphasised** in the advertisement?*

What does it mean?

To **emphasise** means '*to show the importance of something*', especially in speech or writing. The verb '*to stress*' (see Unit 6) has a similar meaning in this context.

When speaking, simply saying one word more loudly or **emphatically** can **emphasise** that word and show that this is the most important word in the sentence.

In an article or conversation, **emphasis** can depend on frequency (how many times something is mentioned), description (the adjectives attached to something) and tone (the feelings and level of formality created by the choice of words).

How to answer:

The advertisement is trying to sell property in country villages to wealthy retired people and new families who may be tired of the noise and the stress of the city. For this reason, *it **emphasises** the peace and tranquility of village life by mentioning the little sounds like the postman's bicycle bell and the bees buzzing around the flowers. The advert also refers to 'the gentle pace' of village life and lists the traditional countryside activities available to help villagers relax in their spare time.*

Be Careful!

This is a common question format in C1 exams. Sometimes the answer might be obvious but very often it can be quite tricky: at C1 level, you may have to do more than simply look for obvious words or synonyms in the text. It's more likely that the answer will be 'suggested' rather than explicit. Look at the example answer above: the basic answer is 'peace and tranquility' but probably these words are not in the advertisement you have to read, and maybe there aren't even any synonyms (like 'quiet' and 'calmness'). More likely, you have to think about *why* the advertisement mentions sounds like bees buzzing and bells chiming and *what* that helps to emphasise about village life. In other words, you may have to make an 'analytical leap' in order to get the answer from the text.

5. Features

Example:

*Choose one of the energy-saving devices shown in the advertisement and say why you might use it yourself. In your answer, you should say what **features** attracted you to the product and what kind of person you would recommend the product to.*

What does it mean?

A **feature** is an interesting or special 'part' of something bigger.

Feature is a very general word: a **landscape feature** might be a river or a rocky outcrop; a **facial feature** might be a cleft chin or a scar; a **magazine feature** might be a special article in a magazine.

The example task above concerns **product features.** Product features are the parts of the product design which make the product useful, special, or attractive.

How to answer:

*I would probably choose the solar-powered phone charger because I use my phone every day and I live in a sunny country. The most useful **feature** of the product for me is the special clip which means you can fix the solar panel to the top of your backpack. There is also a **feature** that lets you stand the panel like a picture on a window ledge. I would recommend this product to students as they use backpacks and phones all the time!*

Be Careful!

1. A **feature** is one part of something bigger, not the whole thing: a <u>facial</u> feature is a long nose or a bushy eyebrow - not an unusual face.

You should NOT say '*a key **feature** of this phone charger is that it charges phones*'. However, you CAN say '*a key **feature** of this phone charger is that it charges phones <u>in under one minute</u>*'.

2. A **feature** does not have to be physical (it can be a personality trait or a style of communication, for example) but it should be specific and directly related to the subject..

You should NOT say '*a key **feature** of this holiday package was that we had a good time*'. However, you CAN say '*a key **feature** of this holiday package was that the hotel staff <u>personalised the service</u> to make sure that we had a good time*'.

3. If a song or show **features** a person or a special thing, it means that a person or thing plays an important part in the song or show: '*The rock song **features** a full string orchestra*'.

6. Illustrate

Example:

*How does the example of the donkey **illustrate** the psychologist's main point?*

What does it mean?

To **illustrate** means literally '*to draw/paint*' (*a picture*).
In formal, analytical 'exam speak', **illustrate** means '*give an example of*' or '*help to explain*', or simply '*show*'.

How to answer:

The psychologist uses the anecdote of the donkey to explain the way that many bosses think about their workers. The traditional idea is that to make the donkey work, the owner must either encourage the donkey with a carrot or force the donkey to move by beating it from behind with a stick. The psychologist then asks what the owner should do if the donkey is working well without carrot or stick. Of course, in this situation, the owner should do nothing and simply step back and let the donkey work. Unfortunately, some bosses seem unable to do this and insist on micromanaging their workers, often to the detriment of the workers' performance.

Be Careful!

1. Make sure you don't simply repeat the language used in the exam text/recording in your answer - if the question asks 'how' you should explain <u>how</u> and add some analysis.

2. The other main variation of this question used in exams is '*What example helps to **illustrate** the psychologist's main point?*' (*Answer: the donkey*)

7. Innate

Example:

*Do you think leadership qualities can be taught or are they **innate**?*

What does it mean?

Innate means '*essential*' or '*an essential part or quality*' of something. '*Essential*' is often used figuratively to mean 'very important' (*It is essential that students revise before the exam*) but in fact, '*essential*' really means '*fundamental*' or '*the most* *defining part/quality of something'.* Indeed, the word *'essence'* comes from the Latin verb *'to be'.*

Similarly, the word **innate** comes from the Latin *'to be born in/with'.* So quite literally, an **innate quality** is one you are born with, rather than something you learn. This **dichotomy** (opposition between two things in an argument or theory) is often referred to as the 'nature versus nurture' debate: How much of our knowledge and behaviour are we born with (nature) and how much is dependent on the influences from our environment as we grow up (nurture)?

How to answer:

*The idea that some people are 'born leaders' has a long and complex history in terms of mythology, psychology, and sociology. It definitely makes for a good story, and powerful individuals usually like to claim that success is a result of their own abilities rather than any social or material advantages they may have enjoyed. On the other hand, 'rags to riches' tales may also be held up as examples that prove leadership is so **innate** a quality, even poverty cannot hold it back.*

However, leadership and material success are not necessarily the same thing. True leadership, many people argue, is displayed only in the most demanding situations such as in times of war or catastrophe, or in the unsung heroes of more everyday roles in challenging areas such as in special needs teaching or community work. Other people see leadership primarily in sporting and adventurous arenas - captaining a yacht on stormy seas, for example, or leading a team of climbers to a coveted first ascent of a formidable mountain route.

Ultimately, it seems that the idea of leadership has a talismanic quality that makes it hard to define in exact, scientific terms. Certainly some individuals seem to have more of a natural capacity for leadership but then again there are lots of different types of leadership, and perhaps more importantly, the desire to lead isn't always the best leadership quality!

Be careful!

1. **Innate** is possibly rather a C2 level word but it does seem to be a favourite in the IELTS exam and may be used together in a question with **to what extent**: *To what extent do you think leadership qualities are innate?* This simply means: *How much do you think leadership qualities are innate or not?*

2. Most of the time, the adjective **innate**, like *fundamental* is not used with intensifiers like *very*: something is either *innate* or *not innate*.

3. In descriptions, the adjective **innately**, may be used:

*Migratory bird species are able to navigate extraordinary distances **innately**.*

8. Outcome

Example:

*According to the writer, which **outcome** would be best for the people of the village?*

What does it mean?

Outcome means 'result' or 'conclusion' and is often used to talk about legal and political results, or to talk about results in a formal, bureaucratic way. Often an **outcome** is more than simply 'the numbers' and also involves a basic description of why the result is significant, and for whom.

How to answer:

The writer is clearly on the side of the villagers, and supports the idea of a road tunnel for the section of the proposed new road that will pass the village to the west. She argues that although this plan is the most costly option, it is necessary to preserve the beautiful views that make the village so special for both the residents and the many tourists who keep local businesses going.

Be careful!

1. Don't confuse **outcome** with '*income*' and '*outgoings*', which refer to money coming in and going out!

2. The word **outcome** (result) is connected to the idioms:

*The thing that **came out** of the event was… (what we learned was)*
*It will all **come out** in the end (we will all discover the truth eventually)*

9. Significance *and* Relevance

Example:

*What **significance** does the colour green have for the guest on the radio show?*

-----

*According to the book extract, what **relevance** does ancient philosophy have to modern life?*

What does it mean?

Significance means '*importance*' and is often used to talk about an important connection.

Relevance means '*connection*' and is often used to talk about an important connection, especially an application - when one thing can be useful in another context.

How to answer:

The radio guest mentions that green is the colour of his local football team and so he always associates green shirts and scarves with memories of going to watch football matches with his father.

In the book extract, the writer makes the argument that the basic principles identified by ancient philosophers should be treated as a practical guide for today's problems, rather than simply a branch of history or a special interest. In particular, the writer argues that modern society has lost a basic understanding of the key principles and issues involved in forming and maintaining a successful and just system of government.

Be careful!

Significance and **Relevance** also have similar adjective and negative forms:

Significant, relevant (adjective)
Insignificant, irrelevant (negative adjective)
Insignificance, irrelevance (negative noun)

Note that **insignificant** means '*unimportant, minor*' while **irrelevant** means '*not important to this issue, not connected to this discussion.*'

10. Summarise

Example:

*Write a short **summary** (between 80-120 words) of the report, including key points, challenges, and recommendations.*

What does it mean?

A **summary** explains everything a reader in a hurry needs to know - the most important information, in just a few sentences or paragraphs (depending on the original amount of text/information) To write a summary, you need to use your judgement to identify the most important information and then re-write it in an economical way (no extra details or opinions).

How to answer:

The report details the current plans, problems, and recommendations concerning the leisure facilities available in the student village. Plans focus on a proposed new sports centre and café-bar which will be partly underground to avoid spoiling the view. Challenges include providing temporary housing for students while the work is completed and making sure this ambitious project does not go over budget. A key recommendation is that the major work should take place during the summer months to minimise disruption. It is further recommended that a full-time project manager from the university's own staff be appointed to work alongside the private contractors.

Be Careful!

1. **Summarising** is a practised skill - you should learn how to do it and practise writing **summaries** in your native language, ideally with advice from an expert or a writing guide. Many exam candidates provide poor summaries because they have not properly learned about, or practised making summaries, in any language.

2. **Summarising** is NOT 're-writing the text in simple language' (paraphrasing). It is NOT 'telling a story from your perspective'. It is <u>identifying and relating the basic situation, and the most important questions, issues, and points</u>, objectively, without extra detail or secondary opinion.

3. It is possible in the C1 exam that you will be given a writing task with more than one instruction: you may be asked to summarise AND give your opinion, or summarise ONLY the *results* of a particular event or situation. You should practise answering official exam questions as part of your exam preparation, and always read the question carefully and follow ALL the instructions.

UNIT 2: TEST!

Fill in the gaps using the keywords from this unit

1. What the tragedy also _____ is the extent to which neighbours nowadays barely know one another.

2. The local police force is _____ the rise in smuggling with extra patrols and trained sniffer dogs.

3. So-called 'soft skills' arguably have greater _____ nowadays in an era of consensus politics and multipolar diplomacy.

4. Residents' objections were _____ in a specially-convened town hall meeting.

5. The Kingfisher can easily be _____ by its dazzling blue and orange plumage.

6. Key _____ of the transport plan include a subsidy for rural routes and free weekend travel for all children.

7. It was only when the old lady took the vase on a TV antiques show, that the true _____ of the item was revealed.

8. _____ doctors, national pressure on health services could be halved if everyone stopped smoking and followed a healthy diet.

9. Due to the football match running into extra time, the nightly news programme was delayed, and the newsreader simply _____ the day's main events in a five-minute bulletin.

10. At this stage, the final _____ is unclear. However, Mrs Parker remains optimistic she will get a good settlement.

11. _____ to all dogs is the ability to identify and track other animals by their scent.

12. The teacher considered it important to _____ the difference between rules and good practice.

Answers: 1. *illustrates* 2. *tackling* 3. *relevance* 4. *addressed* 5. *distinguished* 6. *features* 7. *significance* 8. *According to* 9. *summarised* 10. *outcome* 11. *Innate* 12. *emphasise*

Congratulations! You've completed 20% of your essential exam vocabulary revision for the C1 exam!

UNIT 3: B2 LEVEL MISTAKES

The following ten words and phrases are all essential because they are used so often in everyday English. For this reason they are taught at B1/B2 level, but C1 level learners frequently use them incorrectly in the C1 exam.

Even very confident C1 speakers frequently make mistakes with these words and phrases, often without realising.

Repeated mistakes with important B2 level vocabulary will show the examiner that your level is possibly **below B2**. This is why it is **essential that you check your understanding, and practise** this key vocabulary, to make sure you get it right in the C1 exam.

1. Be used to

Example:

I don't mind getting up early because I **am used to** *it.*
I **am used to** *getting up early so I don't mind it.*

NOT

~~I am used to get up early~~

What does it mean?

Verb 'to be' + used to + noun/Verb-ing means 'experienced with'/ 'accustomed to'.

'**Be used to**' is the most typical way that English speakers describe habits or routines or regular experiences that have become 'normal' over time. It also has the sense of *'this is easy/not a huge problem for me, because I have done it regularly/experienced it for a long time.'*

In the negative *'I* **am not used to** *getting up early'*, the phrase describes a new experience or new routine which is difficult because it is new, strange, and unfamiliar.

'Get used to' and *'getting used to'* are used to describe the process of a new experience or routine becoming less new and difficult, and more normal and bearable.

How to answer:

Use '**be used to + something/someone/V-ing**' in discussions about routines/everyday experiences which are normal/not normal for you compared to other people.

Be Careful!

Learners often confuse *'be used to'* (familiar with) and *'used to'* (past action). There are hundreds of practice exercises available online which will help you to recognise the difference! Search online for *'be used to and used to exercises'*.

After '**be used to**', the next word must be either a noun phrase (*the hot weather/small dinners/it/him*) or a Verb-ing form (*getting up early, finishing work late, eating quickly*).

The Verb-ing form after '*be used to*' seems strange for learners because the '*to*' makes learners think of the infinitive verb form. However, the infinitive must <u>not</u> be used after '*be used to*':

I am used to ~~finish~~ work late.
I am used to finishing work late. ✓

2. Delicious

Examples:

The meal we ate in the local café was **delicious**.
My grandfather makes a **delicious** wine from his own grapes.

NOT

The meal we ate in the local café was very **delicious**. *
Do you have a **delicious** wine we could try, please? *

*These two usages are not 'wrong' in the formal sense, but they sound un-natural in English.

What does it mean?

We all know what '**delicious**' means - tasty food and drink! The problem is the way the word is used. At C1 level, learners need to show a greater understanding of how words are typically used by native speakers.

How to answer:

Use the word '**delicious**' on its own – no basic modifiers or intensifiers like 'very', 'quite'...

...however, you can use 'absolutely delicious' or 'simply delicious' to create an extreme adjective form.

In specific situations, you can also use comparative forms: least, more, and most delicious, for comparing dishes which are all delicious.

Be Careful!

The main problem with the word 'delicious' is that it is terribly over-used by B2 and C1 speakers. This is fine at B2 level, but at C1 level you should demonstrate a wider vocabulary. There are some synonyms:

Mouth-watering
Very more-ish (informal)
A taste to remember

But even better are descriptions of the particular food or drink:

A cool/fruity/full-bodied/rich/sweet/light/delicate/complex/red/white wine
A succulent steak
A refreshing fruit salad
A deliciously spicy curry
A fresh, crisp salad
An aromatic seafood dish

3. For example

Examples:

I do many things to maintain my fitness - **for example**, *cycling to work, walking to the shops, and swimming and football at weekends.*

Are you doing enough to reduce household waste? **For example**, *do you avoid products which come with excessive packaging? Do you compost organic matter? How much food do you throw away, that could have been eaten?*

Some pets, like cats, **for example**, *largely look after themselves, but other animals may demand much more care and attention.*

What does it mean?

You probably know what this means! '**For example**' is used to introduce a specific example (or a list of specific examples) of a statement, claim, or abstract idea.

How to answer:

In the examples above, you can see three different ways of using 'for example' in a sentence.

Be Careful!

The mistake learners make is to confuse the subtitle format '*example(s)*' with the phrase '*for example*'. In a presentation or report, you may want to make a subtitle '**examples**' like this:

Report on the college litter problem

Introduction

A general increase in the amount of litter, mainly food and drinks packaging, scattered around the grounds of the college, has led to complaints from visitors and local residents. There is also concern about health and safety and also the lack of social responsibility shown by students.

Examples

- *Plastic drinks bottles and cigarettes outside the main entrance*
- *Paper waste and plastic bags on the playing fields*
- *Discarded takeaway trays with traces of rotting food*

...

In sentences however, you should use '*for example*'.

You can also use variations like '*one example of this is….*', '*a very good example is…*', '*one unusual example can be found in..*', but in sentences you should not use '*example*' on its own to introduce an example.

4. Fun *and* Funny

Example:

*We had a lot of **fun** yesterday; we played in the park and told lots of **funny** jokes.*

What does it mean?

'Fun' is a noun which means '*good times*', '*enjoyment*' or an adjective which means 'enjoyable', 'light-hearted.
'Funny' is an adjective but it is NOT the adjective form of 'Fun'.
'Funny' usually means '*comical*' and describes comical things which make people laugh.

How to answer:

*A **fun** person likes to play or party. A **funny** person is good at telling jokes and making people laugh.*

Be Careful!

'Funny' has another meaning, synonymous with '*unusual*', '*strange*', or even '*suspicious*'. You must consider the context (the whole situation and other sentences).

*'I did find it **funny** that he never replied to my email'* (It was strange for me).
*'I did find it **funny** when Martin fell into the swimming pool'* (I found it amusing).

5. In common (with)

Examples:

*I have a lot **in common with** my mother: we both like romantic films, walks in the countryside, and dark colours - and we both hate shopping!*

*My mother and I have a lot **in common**: we both like romantic films, walks in the countryside, and dark colours - and we both hate shopping!*

*Despite initially being attracted to one another, Jo and Chris finished dating after realising they didn't have anything **in common** apart from a love of good food and wine.*

In common with *other traditional beers, Mark's popular homebrew is not filtered, lending it a distinctive taste and appearance.*

What does it mean?

'In common with' means 'the same' or 'shared', when two people or things are similar in some way or ways, or 'share' certain characteristics.

How to answer:

Use mainly for comparing the personalities, backgrounds, and likes/dislikes of two people.

Be Careful!

On its own, the word '**common**' has other meanings:

1. Standard everyday practice *(hip replacement surgery is one of the most **common** procedures undertaken by health services).*
2. The most populous of a certain type of plant or animal *(the **common** garden thrush)*
3. Public land or civic space shared by a group of people *(Wimbledon **Common**; the college **common** room)*
4. Proletariat, unsophisticated, ill-mannered *(His table manners were considered very **common** and unrefined)*

6. Look forward (to)

Examples:

*I am **looking forward to** the end of my exam period! (+ noun)*
*I am **looking forward to** finishing my exams (+ V-ing)*
*I **look forward to** the close of the academic year (formal)*
*We were **looking forward to** Christmas (narrative, past continuous)*

*We **looked forward to** Christmas every year (narrative, past simple)*

What does it mean?

'***Look forward to***' means to think about a future time or event in a positive way.

How to answer:

In letters and emails:

Use present continuous for informal (*I am **looking forward to** meeting again*)
Use present simple for formal (*I **look forward to** our next meeting*)

Be Careful!

Always use the three words: ***look + forward + to***
Always follow either with a noun-phrase OR a V-ing form.

Do NOT follow with a Verb infinitive: ~~*I am looking forward to meet you again*~~

7. Until

Examples:

1. *We played tennis **until** it went dark.*
2. *The alarm continued to sound **until** finally the batteries wore out.*
3. *Go to your room and stay there **until** I say you can come out!*
4. *We weren't able to go outside **until** the storm had passed.*
5. ***Until** recently, 'craft beers' were only really popular with old men.*

What does it mean?

1. *We stopped playing tennis when it went dark.*
2. *The alarm stopped when the batteries wore out.*
3. *You can come out of your room when I say.*
4. *We were able to go outside once the storm had passed*

5.   *Recently, 'craft' beers have become very popular with people of all ages.*

'Until' means *'continued in this way to a certain point in time'.*

How to answer:

Use **'until'** to emphasise what happened BEFORE the change.

Be Careful!

In spoken English, **until** is often shortened to **'til:**

*We played tennis **'til** it went dark.*

The meaning is the same.

8. Sympathetic

Examples:

*Mary had a bad day at work but fortunately her husband was very **sympathetic** and made her a nice cup of tea in her favourite mug, listened to his wife's complaints, and made supportive comments.*

*Although the teacher was usually very strict, she was **sympathetic** towards students as they prepared for their exams and allowed them extra time to complete their homework during this period.*

*Margaret was not a member of the socialist party, but she was **sympathetic** to the cause.*

What does it mean?

The adjective **'sympathetic'** means *'considerate/understanding/caring'.*

How to answer:

Use '**sympathetic**' to describe somebody who shows consideration and understanding, especially when somebody is having a bad time or struggling with something.

Be Careful!

Other European languages use the related word '*simpatic*', which rather means '*nice*' or '*personable*', or '*easy to get along with*'. The loanword '*simpatico*' is in some English dictionaries but is not widely used in English.

'**Sympathetic**' should not be confused with '*simpatico*'. ' **To sympathise with**' means rather to feel sorry for someone or to indirectly support someone or something; '*simpatico*' means to have an affinity or shared understanding - '*to be on the same wavelength*'. The two words are related but not used in exactly the same way.

9. Whether

Example:

*I really didn't know **whether** to attend the wedding or make an excuse.*
***Whether** I wanted to or not, I always went with my parents to their ballroom dancing club.*
***Whether** the weather was clement or not, Martin would take his evening walk at seven precisely.*
*Do you know **whether** food is included with the ticket price?*

What does it mean?

'**Whether**' has the logical sense of '*either*', '*this or that*' or '*yes or no*'.

How to answer:

Use '**whether**' to express a choice between (usually two) options or possibilities.

Be Careful!

Don't confuse **'whether'** (yes or no) with:

1. Weather (rain, sun, wind, snow)
2. Wether (a male sheep - the word 'bellwether' meaning '*leader*' or '*early indicator*' comes from this)

10. Work *and* Workplace

Example:

Where do you **work**?
Where is your **workplace**?

What does it mean?

Where do you **work**? = *what is the name of your company/employer?*
Where is your **workplace**? = *what is the geographic location/address of your company?*

How to answer:

A: Where do you **work**?
B: I **work** *at KGH Legal Services*

A: Where is your **workplace**?
B: My **workplace** *isn't in the main office; it's in a business park out of town.*

Be Careful!

- '*At my work*' is considered slang/informal or simply bad English. It is sometimes used, but is not considered 'good' English.
- '*In my work/in my line of work*' means '*in my role/in my industry/in my profession*'.
- The word **'work'** has many different meanings and is used in numerous phrasal verbs and idioms, such as '*work something out*', '*work well together*', '*doesn't work*' and so on.
- '*Safety at work*'/'*Safety in the workplace*' can both be used. There can be a difference in meaning: '*at work*' means '*when you are doing your*

job'; '*in the workplace*' means a building specifically used for a certain job. A police officer can be '*at work*' on the street, but a police officer's **workplace** is the police station.

UNIT 3 TEST!

Fill in the gaps using the keywords and phrases from this unit

1. Billy had spent the night partying and his mother was not very _____ the next day when he complained about having a headache.
2. Geoff has been _____ in the music business for over twenty years, mainly as a producer, although sometimes he performs as a session guitarist.
3. Helen came from a small village in the countryside, so she _____ the fast pace and huge scale of the big city.
4. I have a lot of cousins but I rarely contact them. I've met them several times in the past but we don't have much _____ and so there isn't much to talk about.
5. I love my job but the _____ is terrible: really old-fashioned desks, not enough space, and an ugly dining area.
6. The children will finish school for the summer in two weeks and they are really _____ being on holiday and playing in the sunshine.
7. I plan to keep working _____ I can retire on a full pension.
8. The party was a lot of _____ , everybody had a great time.
9. Not everyone likes your jokes, Harold. _____, Kate was quite offended when you told that story at her party last week.
10. I watched a really _____ film last night; it had me laughing so much I had to wipe away the tears from my face.
11. Susan couldn't decide _____ she wanted a hamburger or a pizza for lunch.
12. The chicken we had for dinner was simply _____.

Answers: 1. *sympathetic* 2. *working* 3. *wasn't used to* 4. *in common* 5. *workplace* 6. *looking forward to* 7. *until* 8. *fun* 9. *For example* 10. *funny* 11. *whether* 12. *delicious*

Congratulations! You've completed 30% of your essential exam vocabulary revision for the C1 exam!

UNIT 4: CONNECTORS

Connectors are words or phrases like *'but'*, *'however'*, *'because'*, *'for example'*, and *'even so'*. These are words and phrases which 'connect' ideas from the previous statement or paragraph to the next statement or paragraph, in a variety of meaningful ways.

Using meaningful connectors adds cohesion (togetherness/structure) to a conversation or written text, and the sense of a well-articulated argument that builds to a logical conclusion. Exam markers are told to look for this quality.

Even more crucially for anyone taking the C1 exam, connectors are a basic requirement for formal writing tasks like essays, reports, and formal letters/emails - put simply: **if you don't use at least some connectors in a formal writing task, you will not get a C1 grade for your answer.**

At B2 level, it is enough to structure writing tasks using the basic *'firstly, secondly, thirdly, finally'* format (or *'first, second, third, finally'* for US English). At C1 level, this format might just be enough, as long as everything else in your answer is great - but if you really want to demonstrate C1 or C1+ ability, you need to **correctly use a range of C1 level connectors.** This unit shows you how to use ten important connectors at C1 level.

1. Accordingly

Example:

*This summer has brought some of the best weather in years to the UK with crowds of people flocking to parks and beaches up and down the country. **Accordingly,** ice-cream sellers and air-conditioning suppliers have reported record sales.*

What does it mean?

'Accordingly' means *'for the same reason'.*

How to answer:

The easiest way to use **'accordingly'** is as a connector at the beginning of a sentence, to describe something that 'matches up with' the previous sentence or paragraph.

Be Careful!

There are other forms with related but different meanings:

'According to' (See Unit 2) ('what somebody/something says or believes)
'In accordance with' (in agreement with a rule or custom)
'Accord' (noun) (a formal, usually political/diplomatic agreement)
'Accord' (verb) (to give somebody an official right, power, or privilege)

2. For this reason

Example:

During monsoon season, travel is often disrupted by heavy rain and flooding. **For this reason**, *journeys are often completed in stages, using whatever transport is available in the moments when the roads are clear.*

What does it mean?

'**For this reason**' means '*because of this*'

How to answer:

Use **'for this reason'** to say what happens as a result of the previous sentence or paragraph

Be Careful!

The 'reason' must be clear in the sentence or paragraph which comes before:

'*After lunch, we took a walk in the old town. ~~For this reason, we didn't take our coats.~~*'

'*After lunch, we took a walk in the old town, <u>which was very close to the hotel.</u> For this reason, we didn't take our coats.*' ✓

(We didn't take our coats because we knew we could quickly return to the hotel if we started feeling cold or if it started to rain).

3. Furthermore

Example:

The new centre for the Arts will provide the city with a much-needed venue for art exhibitions and dramatic performances. **Furthermore***, it will provide an extra incentive for people to move to the area, as part of the wider effort to reduce the long-term decline in local population.'*

'Children should not use bad language; **furthermore***, they should be taught to respect their elders!'*

What does it mean?

'Furthermore' usually means *'and another reason/effect is…'*
'Furthermore' can also mean *'more importantly…'* or *'secondly'*

How to answer:

Use **'furthermore'** in formal debating/presenting language to add an extra 'further' reason or effect of the previous sentence or paragraph, especially when talking about plans, proposals, arguments, strategies, and official orders.

You can also use **'furthermore'** to emphasise a second important point, order, or opinion.

Be Careful!

'Furthermore' should NOT be used simply to add *'the next thing'* or *'the next event'* in a list:

First of all, we visited the beach. After that, we had lunch. Furthermore*, we had a look round the museum.
(*This isn't *necessarily* wrong – native speakers might say this to emphasise an item in a list, or to achieve a particular formal or ironic effect, but it is tricky to get right and so should be avoided in the C1 exam.)

4. In the same way

Example:

Supermarkets have long positioned complementary products alongside each other, like salsa dipping sauce next to potato chips. **In the same way***, webshops present customers with similar products to the one(s) they have chosen, to try to get the extra sale just as the customer is about to pay.*

What does it mean?

Here, **'way'** means *'method'* or *'how something is done/how something happens'*. **'In the same way'** means *'using the same method'* or *'by the same principle/process'*.

How to answer:

Use **'in the same way'** to make a comparison between two similar methods or processes.

Be Careful!

'Way' can also literally mean a *'route'*, *'path'*, or *'road'*. The equivalent phrase for this meaning is **'by the same way'**:

'We got home **by the same way** *that we had been shown by the taxi driver earlier that day.'*

5. In other words

Example:

A recent study concluded that having a family or personal connection to a company or organisation resulted in a 40% higher chance of securing a position. **In other words***, it's not always what you know, but rather who you know that decides professional success.*

What does it mean?

'In other words' means *'another way of saying this is...'*

How to answer:

Normally, '**in other words**' is used after a detailed or technical example, and introduces a much simpler statement, often one which identifies an underlying principle or **aphorism** (general truth) behind the detailed example.

Be Careful!

'In other words' may be used to give a simple definition, rather like '*that is*':

> *The two countries operated on a quid pro quo basis; that is, they co-operated only in the expectation of getting a definite return.*'

..however, '**in other words**' normally comes before some extra analysis and often some irony:

> *The two countries operated on a quid pro quo basis; **in other words**, their 'friendship' was more business than personal.*'

6. One example of this is

Example:

It's true that more and more people are getting worried about smartphone overuse, and we are starting to see a reaction against smartphone overuse. **One example of this is** *the 'phone locker-box' invention, a box for your smartphone which only opens after a programmed amount of time - so you can't use it during a meal, for example, or during a music concert - or while you are sleeping!*

What does it mean?

The pronoun **'this'** connects the previous 'general topic' to your brilliant real-life example!

How to answer:

This is a very useful connector because it reminds you to <u>give real-life examples when you are discussing general topics, trends, or ideas</u>. You can use 'One example of this' in writing tasks but it is also very useful in collaborative speaking tasks (speaking with a partner), when you are given a topic to discuss.

Be Careful!

Don't forget the verb 'to be' for introducing 'the example' as a noun phrase:

*'...One example of this **is** the new wave of mobile apps...*

Or, you can add in some extra information first, using a different verb:

*'...One example of this **can** probably be found in your pocket: the new wave of mobile apps...'*
*'...One example of this **gets** straight to the heart of the issue: the new wave of mobile apps...'*

7. So what I mean is

Example:

*I like eating out in terms of the experience rather than the eating... **So what I mean is**, I enjoy the culture and the conversation more than the food itself.*

---

*I think old people should go to care homes because they are difficult to look after ...**So what I mean is**, when old people need special medical care every day, sometimes a special care home is the only realistic option.*

What does it mean?

'So what I mean is' is a quicker, informal way of saying *'let me explain what I just said in a clearer/more appropriate way.'*

How to answer:

Use '**so what I mean is**' mainly in spoken English to correct yourself or repeat a statement in a clearer or more appropriate or more persuasive way.

'**So what I mean is**' is sometimes used in written English to create an informal, thoughtful, confiding tone.

Be Careful!

The Verb-2 form of '**mean**' is irregular:

*'What I **meant** was...'*

The Verb-3 form is also '**meant**' - this is only really used in the passive:

*'What is **meant** by the phrase: 'a bird in the hand'...?*

8. Surprisingly however,

Example:

Most people can remember their favourite school teacher, with nostalgic recollections typically peppered with comments like 'kind', 'funny', 'made lessons fun', and so on. We naturally imagine that children today value the same qualities most highly in their teachers.

***Surprisingly however**, children nowadays are much more likely to say that it is important for a teacher to be strict but fair. Of course, children want their teachers to be kind, creative, and interesting, but more than anything else, it seems children want clear boundaries and enforcement of good behaviour.*

What does it mean?

'**Surprisingly however,**' means '*...but actually, the opposite is/was true*'.

How to answer:

Use '**surprisingly however**' to highlight a surprising contrast between an expected result and the actual result.

Be Careful!

To use '**surprisingly however**', the first statement must be connected to the second statement by a contrast between '*expectation*' and '*result/reality*'.

> *Mark Wiggins has been a professional stuntman for over twenty years.*
> **Surprisingly however**, *he has never broken a bone in his body.* ✓
> (Everybody expects stuntmen to suffer injuries; it is surprising if they don't)

> *Mark Wiggins has been a professional stuntman for over twenty years.*
> ~~**Surprisingly however**, *he is retiring next year.*~~
> (Incorrect use of connector. There is nothing in the first sentence to make the reader <u>surprised</u> that Mark Wiggins is retiring next year.)

> *Mark Wiggins has been a professional stuntman for over twenty years.*
> **However**, *he is retiring next year.* ✓
> (The basic connector 'however' is correct here, as it highlights the basic contrast between '*working*' and '*retiring*'.)

9. Ultimately, it comes down to

Example:

Choosing the right university is a challenge for many prospective undergraduates. Being in a vibrant city is highly valued by most students, as is belonging to a famous, respected institution. Increasingly, students expect high-quality accommodation as well as teaching and study facilities. **Ultimately, it comes down to** *a simple question: where am I most likely to fit in and do well?*

Deciding on a final winner for best young chef is always difficult: all the young people have worked so hard for months or even years to get to this stage but **ultimately it comes down to** *one dish and one final day in the kitchen.*

What does it mean?

'**Ultimately**' means '*in the end*', '*finally*', or '*basically/at the most basic level*'.

'**Ultimately, it comes down to**' adds emphasis to the idea of '*the most important moment/ the most basic principle*.

How to answer:

Use '**ultimately, it comes down to**' after a list, a detailed description of a problem or issue, or a description of a build-up to a climactic event. Follow the phrase with what you think is the most important underlying point in a topic, or the most important 'moment of truth' in a story.

Be Careful!

The phrase can be modified in a number of ways:

Ultimately, it can come down to (possibly, sometimes)
Ultimately, it may come down to (future possibility)
Ultimately, it came down to (past)
Ultimately, it seems to come down to (roughly speaking, the basic principle/conclusion appears to be this:)
Ultimately, it all comes down to (emphasising the previous description 'all')

10. Which brings me to

Example:

...Of course, not all wealthy people are happy - **which brings me to** *the happiness study mentioned in the article. The study followed hundreds of individuals for their entire lives to find out what it is that makes people happy in the long term. The findings were very clear: strong, meaningful relationships with either friends or family made all the difference to people's happiness, regardless of how rich or poor they were.*

What does it mean?

'**Which brings me to…**' means '*my last point can be explained further by my next point*' or '*my last point introduces my next point*'

How to answer:

Use '**which brings me to…**' when your last point 'opens the door' to your next point - maybe the most important point in your argument.

'**Which brings me to…**' is *semi-formal* - appropriate for articles, debates, and speeches but rather too formal for very casual emails and conversations, and not formal enough for things like job application letters, formal essays, and formal invitations.

Be Careful!

- It can be a bit tricky using the right punctuation with this phrase. The easiest way to use '**which brings me to**…' is after a hyphen (-), as shown in the **example** above.

- '**Which brings me to…**' must be followed by a <u>noun</u> or <u>noun-phrase</u>:

  '*Which brings me to <u>my next/final point</u>, which is that…*'
  '*Which brings me to <u>the most important question</u>: what is the best way to…?*'
  '*Which brings me to <u>Einstein</u>: he is probably the most famous scientist of all time but…*'

- There are some variations:

  '*Which brings **us** to…*'
  '*Which brings me **back** to my original point…*'
  '*We **can** connect lawn tennis to upper-class flirting, which **will** bring us back to Shakespeare's 'A Midsummer Night's Dream' and the idea of 'the garden' as a place of half-wild, physical, natural passion…*'

UNIT 4 TEST!

Fill in the gaps in the following exam-style* essay, using the 'connectors' from Unit 4

Is this the end of 'the rise of the city'?

According to general opinion, human beings are social creatures who prefer to live in communities. (1)_____, many anthropologists argue, the rise of humankind has co-incided with the rise of cities. The infrastructure, security, and versatility afforded by cities allows their citizens to spread risk, manage resources, and invest in specialised skills. (2)_____, we work better together.

(3)_____, the last few years have seen a notable rise in the number of people choosing to live 'off-grid' in remote cabins, often in search of a simpler way of life. (4)_____, growing concern about air pollution in cities has taken the shine off the 'bright lights' of the big city dream, making many people think twice about living in heavily built-up areas. (5)_____ the city of Beijing in China, which is now struggling to attract top international talent. As a young entrepreneur, I can see why.

(6)_____, for the new generation especially, environment and health are much higher priorities. (7)_____, employers are investing much more thought and money into providing 'greener' living and working environments for young, highly-skilled employees.
(8)_____, governments around the world are racing to make their cities cleaner and greener by introducing more electric transport and tougher taxes on fossil fuels - (9)_____ my first point about working together: in my opinion, cities definitely make life easier, more dynamic, and potentially more environmentally friendly too, but only if we co-operate to make city life more pleasant, responsible and healthy.
(10)_____ a simple principle: cities are about living together, so if we want cities to survive, we need to stop asking 'what do I want?' and start asking 'what do we need?'

Answers: (1) For this reason/Accordingly (2) In other words (3) Surprisingly however (4) Furthermore (5) One example of this is (6) So what I mean is (7) Accordingly/For this reason (8) In the same way (9) which brings me back to (10) Ultimately, it comes down to

*The example essay in this exercise is roughly 300 words long. The CAE essay requirement is for 220-260 words, the IELTS requirement for writing task 2 is a minimum of 250 words, while the TOEFL requires a slightly longer essay of 300-350 words. You risk being penalised for writing less than the minimum word requirement, but there is no upper limit (although you will be penalised for writing irrelevant or incoherent material). For a C1 pass-grade, the typical advice is to make sure you write the minimum and don't aim for more than about 15% above the maximum, as quality is more important than quantity, and it is very important that you leave enough time to check your work for mistakes.

Students aiming for a higher level C1+ grade, meanwhile, need to be confident writing slightly longer essays, around 300-350 words in length. Students aiming for a C2 grade should be aiming for an essay length of 350-450 words.

Congratulations! You've completed 40% of your essential exam vocabulary revision for the C1 exam!

UNIT 5: PHRASAL VERBS AND IDIOMS

C1 English learners will know that there are hundreds, even thousands of phrasal verbs in the English language. Many of these verb phrases have multiple meanings in different situations. Unsurprisingly, phrasal verbs can be particularly hard for EFL learners to remember and use with 100% accuracy. Fortunately, examiners realise this and do not mark people down from C1 to B2 for simple mistakes (for example, with prepositions) as long as the intended meaning is still clear.

However, the ability to use a range of phrasal verbs confidently at C1 level will definitely contribute towards a higher mark in the exam.

Most importantly, C1 students should know what certain key phrasal verbs *mean*, in order to understand tasks and questions which might include these phrasal verbs.

Here is a selection of some favourite 'exam' phrasal verbs often used in the kind of analytical/formal tasks and questions you will see in the C1 exam.

1. Get the gist

Example:

*'...After about an hour of listening to a speaker talk about the special techniques for conflict resolution, I thought I had **got the gist**, but soon it would be time to put the training into practice.'*

Question 1: What does the writer mean when she says 'I thought I had got the gist'?

a. *She felt she understood the basic idea*
b. *She felt she was starting to get bored*
c. *She felt she had a detailed understanding*
d. *She felt irritated*

What does it mean?

To **get the gist** means *to understand the main point, theme, principle, setting,* or simply *'what is going on'* generally. If you have **got the gist** (of something), it usually means a situation or idea is fresh or new to you, but you have managed to make some basic sense of it. It does NOT mean you have a detailed or experienced understanding of something.

How to answer:

The correct answer is (a) She felt she <u>understood the basic idea.</u>

*(The speaker had provided enough information to enable the trainees to **get the gist** of the techniques, before trying them out in practice.)*

Be Careful!

1. When speaking, **gist** is pronounced with a **dʒ**, like 'jam' or 'giant'.

2. In the 'EFL world', students may be asked to 'read for **gist**' (read quickly to get the basic idea), 'scan' for information (read very quickly to find a particular piece of information), and 'read for detail' (read part or all of a text very closely to focus on the exact meaning and significance).

3. **Get the gist** is most often connected with speed - getting a quick, initial understanding of a situation or idea. However, it can also take a long time

for someone to **get the gist** if the new information or situation is confusing or alien, or if the person is a bit slow.

2. Get to the heart of (sth)

Example:

When the second speaker says he wants to **'get to the heart of** *the issue', what does he mean?*

a. *He wants to focus on the emotional element*
b. *He wants to rule out the emotional element*
c. *He wants to identify the basic problem or cause*
d. *He wants to talk about the problem in a general way*

What does it mean?

To **'get to the heart of something'** (often a problem or issue) means to find the central, most important point (in the same way the heart is in the centre of the body and also the most essential organ).

How to answer:

The correct answer is (c) He wants to identify the basic problem or cause.

(If we want to **get to the heart of the issue** *of homelessness we need to look at the lack of awareness of and funding for mental health problems and support.)*

Be Careful!

1. **'At the heart of'** can be used to talk about a problem or issue (*at the heart of the problem*), or it can be used to talk about a fundamental principle (innovation is at the heart of our business).

2. 'In the heart of' can be used locationally (*the old pub is located in the heart of the city*), or with a different meaning to talk about 'heartfelt' ideas, beliefs, and memories (*in the hearts of many British people, a bracing walk on a wet windy day followed by a warming cup of tea by the fire is an oddly pleasing thing*).

3. 'At heart' is used to describe a person's true sympathies and means *'essentially'* or *'underneath outward appearances or social training'*: *'At heart, Brian was rather an artist with a sensitive soul, but his experience in business had taught him to wear a mask of cold indifference.'*

3. Play down

Example:

The football match ended in controversy after an on-pitch brawl between up to ten players but the coach of the winning team was quick to **play down** *the incident, dismissing it as nothing more than 'high passions and a bit of pushing and shoving'.*

What does it mean?

To **play down** (something) means to talk about something (usually a problem) in a way that tries to make it seem smaller or less significant.

How to answer:

In any competition, be it in sport, business, politics, love or war, the losers typically draw attention to broken rules, while the winners, happy with the result, tend to **play down** *such transgressions.*

Be Careful!

1. **'Play down'** is most often used in news or magazine articles and usually refers to a public comment designed to reduce public anger or fear.

2. **'Play down'** can also be used when arguing that a person's positive contribution to a project was limited (*I don't want to* **play down** *Mark's useful contribution but the fact remains that it didn't actually solve the problem.*)

3. The phrasal verb **'play down'** has no connection with the general meaning of either 'play' or 'down', for example: *'the midfielder played the ball down the field'* (the midfielder kicked the ball along the length of the pitch).

4. Relate to *and* identify with

Example:

What example does the radio guest give from his own experience in order to show how he relates to children growing up in foreign countries?

What example does the radio guest give from his own experience in order to show how he identifies with children growing up in foreign countries?

What does it mean?

Relate to and **identify with** have a similar phrasal meaning - a shared understanding based on shared experience.

In some contexts they can mean the same thing, but in other contexts there may be a slight difference in meaning: **relate to** can be used to describe a similar experience, while **identify with** is more likely to refer to a very similar or the same experience.

How to answer:

The radio guest refers to his school days as a child from a working-class background sent to a private school attended by children from very wealthy families. He draws parallels between his experience as an 'outsider' and the challenges faced by children who move to a different country. (He relates to them)

The radio guest refers to his own Lebanese background and the fact that, even though he was born and raised in England, he was obviously foreign in appearance compared with the mainly white children in the small town where he grew up. The guest feels his experience is very close to that of children growing up in foreign countries. (He identifies with them)

Be Careful!

1. Don't confuse the phrasal verb '**to relate to**' and the passive phrase 'be related to'!

To relate to a person or experience means *'to understand someone or something because you have had a similar experience'.*

To be related to a person means that two people are part of the same family. Ideas, problems, and topics can also be related (*Climate change is related to population growth*).

2. The phrase ~~to relate well with~~ is used by some speakers to mean '*get on well with/ have a good relationship with*', but this phrase may be considered bad English, and is best avoided in the C1 exam.

3. *To relate* a story or event means to tell a story or give an account of an event.

5. Set the tone

Example:

What word or phrase does the writer use to help **set the tone** *at the beginning of the short story?*

——

The woman says that although the car broke down on her way to the church to get married, she was able to get lift in a fire engine that happened to be passing, meaning that she arrived to her own wedding in a fire engine. What does she mean when she says that this moment '**set the tone** *for the whole day'?*

What does it mean?

'Tone' means '*exact shade or colour*' or '*mood*' or '*style of expression*'.

In the first example above, **set the tone** means '*create a specific mood*'
In the second example, **set the tone** is used more figuratively to mean '*give a certain feeling or theme*'.

How to answer:

The writer uses the word 'officially' in the line 'officially, the verdict was suicide' to suggest that the death is actually an unsolved murder and possibly a cover-up. This immediately sets a cynical, suspicious tone suitable to a crime thriller.

The woman describes turning up to the church in a bright red fire engine as a bizarre but ultimately fun and memorable turn of events and it seems that the whole day continued in this slightly surreal, light-hearted, comic way, with other mishaps providing fun memories rather than real problems.

Be Careful!

Tone is a slippery word that may refer to different shades of a colour, a musical note, a style of speaking, a level of formality, the choice of words in a story to create mood, or the feeling of a formal event.

6. Take (sb/sth) for granted

Example:

To what extent do we **take** *essential natural resources like clean water and fresh air* **for granted***?*

What does it mean?

To **take something for granted** means '*to treat something precious without care and respect*'.

The detailed meaning requires a longer explanation:

The verb **to grant** means formally 'to give', as in '*to grant permission*'.

The adjectives '*given*' and '*granted*' also have the reflected meaning of '*accepted*', and by extension this can mean '*guaranteed*', as in '*we have this*' or '*we know this*' or '*this is guaranteed because we have it in our hands*'. (See **Given that** in Unit 5).

Taken has the phrasal meaning of '*received with a certain understanding or mood*', '*understood in a certain way*' or '*understood as*'

Put these together and you have '*understood as guaranteed*'.

Finally, **taken for granted** is always used negatively to mean *'treated as though it were guaranteed'*, which in turn means *'treated carelessly / unthinkingly / contemptuously / without respect'*.

How to answer:

*By some estimates, up to 30% of clean drinking water is wasted through leaking pipes and irresponsible use, such as leaving taps running or over-watering gardens. At the same time, we routinely use waterways as rubbish dumps for general waste and sewage, as well as highly toxic chemicals. When we consider how essential clean water is to keep humans and other creatures alive, it can only be concluded that we not only **take clean water for granted**, but we are downright reckless in our behaviour - or perhaps simply in denial. Similarly with the issue of clean air, we...*

Be Careful!

In love and relationships, **take someone for granted** has a similar meaning, but with the added element that the one person doesn't expect the other to leave and doesn't make much of an effort to be a good husband/wife/boyfriend/girlfriend:

*'Martin **took his girlfriend for granted**. He always left the housework to her and spent most of his spare time playing computer games on his own. He was surprised when she left him but nobody else was.'*

7. Take (sth) well/badly/to heart

Example:

1. *What does the writer mean when he says his children **took it reasonably well** when he had to explain that their pet rabbit had died?*
2. *Why do some people **take** failure so **badly**?*
3. *Why do some people **take** obviously silly comments to **heart**?*

What does it mean?

The question *'how did he **take** the news?'* means *'how did he react to the news?'* *'what was his immediate reaction?'* *'what effect did the news have on his mood?'* The most obvious answer would be either *'he **took it well**'* or *'**he took it badly**'*.

This phrasal meaning of 'take' is used frequently in English to talk about how one person reacts to news or a special situation (usually bad news, a challenging situation or a joke that mocks that person).

To **take something to heart** describes when a person is deeply affected by something. It often means that a person has heard a general comment or principle and applied this to themselves on a personal level. It might mean that a person is offended personally by a careless comment, or it might mean a person has committed to a certain belief or principle.

How to answer:

1. *The writer means that although the children were naturally upset to hear their rabbit had died, they were quite strong and understanding, and not totally distraught.*
2. *Some people take failure badly because they have grown up in a culture which attaches shame to failure. Others may have a particular emotional insecurity or vanity which makes failure especially hard to bear.*
3. *We shouldn't react to criticism or mocking comments when they are clearly silly, light-hearted, or meaningless. The fact is however, that some people are just more sensitive or passionate than others and may dwell unnecessarily on a thoughtless remark, giving it more significance than it probably deserves.*

Be Careful!

There are numerous phrasal verbs, idioms, and collocations which use 'take'. Some are similar to the meaning shown here (for example: *take offence, take it the wrong way*) and some are very different in meaning (for example: *take off, take a leaf out of my book*).

8. Tend to/Tend towards/Be prone to

Example:

1. *The tourists* **tend to** *cluster mainly around the seafront and the castle; only the more adventurous stray off the beaten track to seek out the more hidden charms of the town.*
2. *The teacher* **tends towards** *a lecturing style, preferring to take questions only at the end of classes.*
3. *The teacher is* **prone to** *going on a bit, which can make the lessons boring.*

What does it mean?

Tend to is used before a verb, to describe a general habit or frequent occurrence which doesn't happen all the time but happens often enough to be 'the norm'.

Tend towards has the same meaning but is used to introduce an abstract noun.

Prone to is used before a noun or Verb-ing form, usually to describe either a *negative tendency* (when someone or something often does something in a negative way), or a vulnerability to a disease (for example: *German Shepherd dogs are* **prone to** *arthritis*).

How to answer:

Use **tend to + Verb** and **tend towards + noun/V-ing** to describe the most typical ways someone or something behaves, or a slight variation in behaviour that happens frequently. The behaviour can be positive or negative or neutral.

Use **prone to + noun/V-ing** to describe a negative variation in behaviour, or a vulnerability to a disease.

Be Careful!

The simple verb **'to tend'** has a totally different meaning - '*look after*' or '*care for*'. This verb may use the preposition 'to' before the object noun:
The nurses tended **to** *the sick and dying soldiers.*

9. Try to work out how

Example:

*Engineers have been **trying to work out how** to reproduce the lab experiment in the real world.*

---

*First of all we must **try to work out how** we can keep the music festival running while respecting local residents' concerns about noise and litter.*

What does it mean?

Try to work out how is a useful, simple way of saying '*attempt to find a solution/answer*'.

How to answer:

Use **try to work out how** as a versatile, less formal construction or a useful way of linking sentences fluently in spoken conversation.

Be Careful!

Try to work out - can be followed by any of the question words (what, which, when, where, who, how). In each combination, the 'try to work out' has the meaning of 'attempting to find the answer' to the particular question.

10. Zero in on (sth)

Example:

*How can psychometric tests help employers to **zero-in on** desirable qualities in potential employees?*

What does it mean?

To **zero-in on** means '*to identify, focus, and concentrate on a specific target*'.

How to answer:

Psychometric testing is an increasingly popular addition to the traditional job interview. By asking questions related to behaviour and a range of everyday issues and hypothetical situations, psychologists claim they can accurately identify and measure crucial characteristics - such as leadership or problem-solving skills - that employers may be looking for in potential employees.

Be Careful!

Zero in on can also be used in a more literal way to talk about a person moving towards a thing or target, or a soldier aiming a rifle at a target.

UNIT 5 TEST!

Fill in the gaps with the phrasal verbs from Unit 5.

1. I think Sarah's comment is really important because it _____ what we want to achieve with this project.

2. Claire didn't fully understand the new computer system but after a bit of practice she was able to _____ and perform most of the basic tasks without a problem.

3. The new teacher found it difficult initially to _____ the schoolchildren because they came from a very different culture to his own.

4. It's understandable that the politician will want to _____ the seriousness of this scandal, but the public will probably demand a full explanation.

5. The film, like most of this director's work, _____ high drama and over-stylised production but is ultimately rescued by strong performances from its lead actors.

6. The main disadvantage of the cheaper machine is that it _____ malfunction in hot conditions.

7. When Kate heard the bad news she _____ and she hasn't come out of her house since.

8. The opening night of the film festival _____ with more serious films than previous years, and stars on the red carpet wore suitably conservative outfits to match the sombre mood.

9. I like her cake recipes but she _____ add too much sugar for my taste.

10. The problem with our marketing campaign is that it is too general in scope; we need to _____ our target market more efficiently and more aggressively.

11. The purpose of the trade forum is to _____ different professionals can work together to provide new solutions.

12. We had a two-day power cut during severe storms last winter and it was only when I had to live without heating in the freezing cold that I realised how much I _____.

Answers: 1. *gets to the heart of* 2. *get the gist* 3. *relate to* 4. *play down* 5. *tends towards* 6. *is prone to* 7. *took it badly* 8. *set the tone* 9. *tends to* 10. *zero in on* 11. *try to work out how* 12. *took it for granted*

Congratulations! You've completed 50% of your essential exam vocabulary revision for the C1 exam!

UNIT 6: DISCURSIVE LANGUAGE

At C1 level, you are expected to discuss ideas (in both speech and writing, but especially in writing) in a **discursive** way. You may be asked to write a **discursive essay**. Certainly, many of the exam texts and questions will be written in a **discursive style**.

What does this mean?

- The word **discursive** has various meanings but all of these in some way refer to a lecturing/essay style which takes a **very broad, formal, and pedestrian (step by step) approach to a topic.**

- A **discursive approach** typically involves looking at the wider topic 'piece by piece', breaking it into subtopics and identifying the main perspectives and issues and moving from one to the next in a methodical way (for academic purposes).

- Additionally, students are usually taught to be objective and to use lots of passive and cleft constructions, qualifiers and formal language, as part of this **discursive style**.

- You probably won't use the pronoun 'I', or give any direct opinions of your own, in a discursive essay or discussion, unless the question specifically asks for your opinion.

- **Discursive language** is not just about a certain choice of words, but also the way words are used in formal academic essays.

Not all academic essays take the discursive approach: the other main approach is the **argumentative approach**, in which you should strongly argue for one perspective or idea, or 'side'. Even in an argumentative essay however, discursive language will still be used because it provides rhetorical (persuasive) options for arguing a case, and simply because it has the desired academic style.

The discursive style has a useful application in the academic world as a means of discussing ideas and presenting complex information in a standardised, unemotional way. In everyday English and non-academic writing however, this discursive style is usually avoided because, outside of the academic world, the discursive style almost always feels verbose, pedantic, excessively formal, boring, artificial, pompous and worst of all: aimless. Indeed, the word **discursive** literally means '*rambling*', which has the figurative meaning of '*talking at length about random subjects to no particular purpose*'.

This is a perfect example of 'exam-speak'. At school and university, below postgraduate level, students spend much of their time constructing formal arguments for no other reason than showing that they can construct formal arguments. This phenomenon is even more apparent in EFL exams at C1 level, in which candidates must be able to talk randomly about any topic, for the sole objective of demonstrating language knowledge and ability: this really is *talking for the sake of talking* (or *writing for the sake of writing*)!

In this way, a *discursive exam task* can be seen as a kind of 'language presentation' or 'technical performance' in which you show off your special discursive language: in real life, you might use one or two of these formal phrases to make a special point in a conversation or email, but outside of a formal academic context it is highly unlikely you will ever subject your friends or colleagues to an entire lecture in the discursive style.

In the artificial world of the C1 exam however, this discursive style should be your default mode in all formal tasks (debating and comparing in speaking tasks, and all formal writing tasks).

This unit takes a selection of verbs and prepositions and shows how they may be used in C1 exam questions. In addition, examples are provided of special sentence structures which show how this vocabulary can be used in a discursive style.

1. Assume

Example:

*According to the speaker, what should we not **assume** about artificial intelligence?*

What does it mean?

To **assume** means '*to accept something as true*' usually without hard evidence, and often on a provisional (temporary) or conditional basis, for the purpose of exploring a possibility or idea.

Assume is an important word in the academic world and is used in three main ways:

1. To distinguish between empirical facts and unproven assumptions.
2. To describe an idea that is not proven, but worth exploring on a hypothetical basis.
3. To describe a temporary role, or to imagine something from a particular position: *'If we were to assume the role of judge and jury, then we would probably hold them guilty.'*

How to answer:

*The speaker suggests that while we might reasonably **assume** that robots will soon take over many jobs currently performed by humans, we shouldn't automatically anticipate 'the end of human labour'.*

Other discursive constructions

- *It can be **assumed** that this trend will continue…*
- *We can **assume** that this trend will continue…*

- *One might **assume** that this trend will continue but surprisingly…*
- *One might reasonably **assume** that this trend will continue, provided that…*

- ***Assuming** that this trend continues, it will be possible to…*
- *If we **assume** this trend will continue, it might be possible to…*
- *If we are to **assume** this trend will continue, then what should…*

Be Careful!

There is a big difference between:

- A conscious assumption (positive: you know you are making an assumption, usually to explore a hypothetical idea, or because no better evidence is available)
- An unconscious assumption (negative: a position of ignorance or prejudice)

2. Associate (with)

Example:

Read the four articles about home-design. Which writers **associate** *high-rise housing* **with** *anti-social behaviour?*

What does it mean?

To **associate** is to group two or more things (or people) together in the mind. It's similar to making a connection, except technically, a connection is more definite - an association is simply two things or people seen or imagined in the same place or in the same idea.

When there is an **association between** two things (for example: *intelligence* and *wearing glasses*), it means that people in general tend to think of intelligence when they think of glasses: *'Many people associate wearing glasses with intelligence'*.

Frequently in an academic context, **associations** deal with psychological and sociological issues.

How to answer:

Writer A and writer C clearly **associate** *high-rise housing with anti-social behaviour. Writer B, on the other hand, identifies street crime as a problem that is connected to* *political decisions. Writer D does not mention either high rise buildings or anti-social behaviour.*

<u>Other discursive constructions</u>

- *It is reasonable to* **associate** *darkness with fear.*
- *We can see why darkness is typically* **associated** *with fear.*
- *It is not hard to see why darkness is typically* **associated** *with fear.*

- *One might choose to* **associate** *darkness with fear.*
- *One might reasonably choose to* **associate** *darkness with fear.*
- ***Associating*** *darkness with fear is something that can be traced back to our prehistoric past.*

Be Careful!

Associate has other meanings:

- An **association** can be an official club of like-minded people or workers who share a trade, for example: *The National Association of Bakers.* In a similar way, an **associate** (noun, pronounced with a schwa for the second 'a') is a business partner.

- If one person **associates with** another person it means those two people meet together more than once, or visit the same social gatherings, more than once. It is a formal way of saying a person spends time in the same place(s) with another person or people, while the exact relationship is unclear.

3. Attribute to

Example:

To what does writer B **attribute** *the decline in home ownership in the UK?*

What does it mean?

To **attribute** *a* to *b*, is to say that *a* is caused or produced by *b*.

In an academic context, **attribute to** is most likely to be used to talk about *cause* and *effect*.

How to answer:

In explaining the possible factors behind lower home ownership rates among younger people, writer B points to the long term increase in enrolment in higher education and also the rises in tuition fees and living expenses borne by students. Writer B goes on to make the basic point that nowadays, a significantly greater proportion of young people are spending more time and more money on higher education, and delaying the purchase of a home as a direct result.

Other discursive constructions

- *This phenomenon can be **attributed to** a rise in greenhouse gas emissions.*
- *We can **attribute** this phenomenon **to** a rise in...*
- *This phenomenon may **be attributed to** a rise in...*

- *If we **attribute** this phenomenon **to** rises in greenhouse gas emissions, we must also conclude that...*

- *This phenomenon has been **attributed to** a rise in...*
- *Scientists have **attributed** this phenomenon **to** a rise in...*
- *Widely **attributed to** a rise in greenhouse gas emissions, this phenomenon has its most obvious effect in the massive storms that have occurred lately with increasing frequency.*

Be careful!

1. Don't confuse the verb **attribute to** with the noun '*a tribute to*'! The noun is usually used to describe musical or other artistic performances which honour a famous musical or other artist by playing or otherwise featuring interpretations of their work. '*The show was billed as a tribute to Shirley Bassey*'.
2. **Attributed to** sometimes has the sense of '*not fully proven*', or '*most experts agree that...*' This sense of the verb is best expressed in the standard treatment of quotes whose origin cannot be accurately determined but are 'widely thought' to have been first said, or at least made famous by a certain person: '*the quote is **attributed to** Winston Churchill*'.
3. **Attributable to** is the adjective form and has the same meaning, for example: '*the phenomenon is attributable to rises in greenhouse gases*'.

4. Concerned with *and* Concerning

Example:

What is paragraph A chiefly **concerned with**?

_____

Concerning *the question of accommodation for the trip, why does speaker A disagree with speaker B?*

What does it mean?

In academic and business English, a **concern** is a *'subject or entity of interest'*.

In this context, to say *a* is chiefly **concerned with** *b*, means that <u>the main focus of *a* is *b*</u>.

(**'Concerning'** + noun) is a way of highlighting a particular focus within a larger topic, or moving on to a new topic or question.

How to answer:

Paragraph A deals mainly with the history of bookmaking.

_____

Speaker A disagrees with Speaker B's insistence on en-suite bathrooms for all the group members on the trip. Speaker A feels that while en-suite bathrooms are preferable, the group should be prepared to be flexible in order to ensure the trip is organised on time and within budget.

<u>Other discursive constructions</u>

- *If we* **concern** *ourselves firstly* **with** *logistics, a number of issues present themselves…*
- *Historically, this topic is* **concerned** *mainly* **with** *the moral aspects…*
- *This essay is* **concerned with** *the various traditional methods of bookmaking…*

- *The history of bookmaking may be approached from the perspective of either the writer or the craftsman.* **Concerning** *the former, it may be observed that the* *earliest 'writers' were often scribes tasked with recording oratory or copying texts...*

Be careful!

The more basic, everyday meaning of **concern**, **concerned** and **to be concerned with** is *'worry'*, *'worried'* and *'to be worried about'*. The difference in meaning depends on the context:

We are concerned with performance (introducing a topic in a discursive essay = the topic is performance)
We are concerned with performance (comment to a factory manager in a meeting or letter = we feel performance is a problem)

5. Considering that *and* Compared to

Example:

Considering that the weather conditions were the worst in ten years, should the tournament be called a relative success?

What does it mean?

The preposition **considering (that)** is used to make a relative opinion: *'he's a good footballer for an amateur = **considering** he's an amateur, he's a good footballer = relative to his amateur level, he's a good footballer'.*

How to answer:

It was a foregone conclusion that the tournament would be less than spectacular this year, with some competitors pulling out before the event and barely half of all tickets sold. However, it must be said that under the circumstances, the organisers did remarkably well to keep the show going and make it as successful as it was: despite the terrible weather and low turnout, the hardcore fans still had a great time and with some of the main competitors absent from the lineup, younger players had a chance to step into the limelight.

<u>Other discursive constructions</u>

- **_Considering_** *the political climate at the time, it seems surprising that anyone would choose to invest in a risky new business…*
- **_Considering_** *that the political climate was so fractious at the time…*
- *It seems surprising that anyone would choose to invest in a risky new business,* **_considering_** *the political climate at the time.*
- *If we* **_consider_** *the political climate of the time, investing in a new business would have been a risky prospect.*

Be careful!

1. Don't confuse **considering that** (relative opinion) and **compared to** (basic comparison/contrast):

Considering (that) she is only five years old, her maths is amazing! ✔

~~*Compared to her age, her maths is amazing!*~~ (You <u>can't</u> compare '*her age*' and '*her maths*').

Compared to that of the average five year old, her maths is amazing! ✔ (You <u>can</u> compare '*the maths of the average five year old*' and '*her maths*').

- 'Compared' can only be used with two similar things. This is why '~~*compared to my brother, my legs are longer*~~' is incorrect. The correct comparison is '*compared to my brother**'s**, my legs are longer.*' (my legs compared to my brother's legs).

2. **Considering** can also be used to simply focus on a subject, or elements of a subject:

"Considering the issue of power shortages first, it seems that…"

"Considering the wider role of the university in the city, the most obvious solution might be to…"

6. Determine

Example:

According to the article, how did the students **determine** *the composition of the water?*

What does it mean?

To **determine** means '*to measure*' or '*to estimate*', usually physical proportions like size and distance.

To **determine** can also mean '*to find out*' or '*to establish*' or '*to specify*', usually in the context of problem solving (for example: '*determine the cause of death*', '*determine the methods used*', '*determine who should do what task*', '*determine who is speaking*' etc.)

How to answer:

We are told that the students were able to **determine** *the composition of the water by using only basic equipment and household chemical products, and the techniques they had learned in class.*

Other discursive constructions

- First, we should begin by **determining** the main factors
- It would be prudent to first **determine** the major factors
- Experts have **determined** three critical factors
- Three critical factors can be **determined**

- If we **determine** the depth of the lake by the new standard, we find that it may be twenty metres deeper than previously estimated.

Be careful!

In everyday language, the most common form and use of this word is the Verb-3 adjective 'determined', which is most often used to describe the feeling or attitude of being committed to a goal ('*she was determined to finish the race*', '*he was a very determined young man*').

7. Exaggerate

Example:

'According to the news reporter, were the initial hurricane reports accurate, or were they **exaggerated?'**

a.   *The initial reports were accurate and not exaggerated*
b.   *The initial reports were inaccurate but not exaggerated*
c.   *The initial reports were inaccurate and exaggerated*
d.   *The initial reports were inaccurate because they underestimated the damage*

What does it mean?

To **exaggerate** means to represent or describe something as bigger, better, worse, or more extreme than it really is. **Exaggerated** is a verb-3 passive adjective.

In everyday, trivial use, **exaggeration** is often identified in stories and anecdotes, sometimes referred to as 'fisherman's tales' (*the fish was bigger than I am!*). Artists may also **exaggerate** certain features in their subjects for the sake of emphasis, composition, or artistic expression.

In journalism, politics, law, and academic use, the word **exaggerate** is most often connected with a search for the truth. Once exaggeration is found and proven, the next question will concern motivation: *who* exaggerated the claim, and *why*?

How to answer?

According to the reporter, the initial reports were inaccurate because there was some confusion about the exact path of the hurricane. Some towns initially described as seriously damaged were later found to be only slightly affected, while other towns not mentioned in the earlier reports were later discovered to have suffered the most severe levels of destruction. The reporter adds that some of the latest, unofficial reports on social networking sites are exaggerating the spread of the damage.

The answer is: *(b) The initial reports were inaccurate but not exaggerated.*

Other discursive constructions

- *To claim Smith's work set the agenda for subsequent writers in the genre would be to* **exaggerate** *the overall significance of her novels. Nonetheless, hers is an important contribution to science fiction and the award is fully justified.*
- *While the overall significance of Smith's work may have been* **exaggerated** *by her most ardent supporters, it cannot be denied that her novels represent an important contribution to science fiction.*
- *It would probably be an* **exaggeration** *to say that Smith's novels set the agenda for science fiction writers, but...*
- *Though clearly* **exaggerated** *by some critics, the significance of her work to the genre of science fiction cannot be denied.*

Be careful!

Exaggeration is a form of untruth that in some situations may be a deliberate lie, but in other situations is simply the product of harmless enthusiasm, boasting, or 'poetic licence' in the dramatic telling of a story. Sometimes it can be somewhere in-between: a 'half lie'; a manipulation or selective retelling of the truth that avoids committing to a full lie. These context-dependent distinctions may be important in choosing the right answer for an exam question.

8. Given (that)

Example:

Given that *the main reason for holding the concert is to promote local talent, what would appear to be the obvious problem with Mark's plan, according to the information?*

What does it mean?

Given that means '*accept this premise as fact*', usually for the purpose of posing a question or problem.

Given that is often used in mathematical questions (*given that $a=12$ and $b=5$, what is the length of c?*)

Given that can also be used in the same way as '**considering/considering that**' (*See 5 in this unit*) to emphasise a certain point and make a relative opinion.

How to answer:

Mark's strategy for promoting local talent would appear to be based on selling tickets for a few internationally-famous performers in order to pull in large crowd numbers. In theory, these large crowds would then also see the smaller, local bands play. Unfortunately however, the big bands are all booked for the Saturday night, while most of the small local bands are due to play on Saturday afternoon and on Sunday. Unless Mark, as concert organiser, makes some last-minute changes to the scheduling, it seems likely the big crowds will only turn up for the Saturday night headliners and not for the smaller bands.

Other discursive constructions

- *Given that lighting - alongside space - is one of the fundamentals of architecture and design, it seems strange that it should so often be overlooked.*
- *It seems strange that lighting should so often be overlooked, especially given that it is acknowledged - alongside space - as one of the fundamentals of architecture and design.*
- *Given the topic, it would be remiss to omit any mention of the role played by lighting.*
- *It would of course be possible to devote an entire thesis to this topic, but Given the summary nature of this essay, we must limit ourselves to the key points.*

Be careful!

1. **Given that** is usually used to emphasise something that is clearly true or arbitrary. If you want to make a more speculative comment, you should use 'assuming that' or 'supposing that'.

2. Be aware of the related phrases '*it's a given that...*' and '*x is a given*', which may be used in a semi-formal way to emphasise something which is, or should be, obvious:

It's a given that some events will always have to be cancelled due to adverse weather conditions/For the purposes of event-planning in the UK, bad weather is practically a given.

9. Stress (sth)

Example:

*What do the safari tour operators **stress** in their advice to customers?*

What does it mean?

In a formal context, the verb **to stress** means *'to emphasise/show the importance of something'*.

How to answer:

In their promotional material, the tour operators make a special point of reminding customers that the wild animals they will be seeing can be dangerous and that customers are responsible for staying inside the vehicle at all times.

Other discursive constructions

- *It cannot be **stressed** enough that these findings are provisional, and further tests will need to be conducted on a larger scale before the new drug can be confirmed as a cure for the disease.*
- *The point to **stress** here is that these are only provisional findings, and the drug will only be confirmed as a cure for the disease provided further tests are successful.*
- *The scientists involved are keen to **stress** that these are only provisional findings...*
- *It should be **stressed** that these are provisional findings: the drug will only be confirmed as a cure for the disease provided further tests are successful.*
- *The scientists **stress** caution in interpreting the results at this preliminary stage.*

Be careful!

Don't confuse with the everyday meaning of *'stress'* meaning *'tension/anxiety/worry'*. Informally, an English speaker might say *'don't stress!'* meaning *'don't worry!'* However, when the verb is used in this way with a direct object, it needs a preposition:

I always stress <u>about</u> money
He's always stressing <u>over</u> little details

When the verb **to stress** is used with a direct object but <u>without</u> a preposition, and in a formal context, the meaning is rather '*to emphasise*'.

*The teacher **stressed** the importance of context.*

10. Support (an opinion, claim, or theory)

Example:

*Which two other writers **support** writer A's claim that emotional intelligence (EQ) is more important than 'hard' intelligence (IQ)?*

(CAE exam, cross-text multiple matching)

----

*In paragraph three, Jackie Bride is quoted to **support***

a.   *The writer's position that older people are better at considering complex ethical problems*
b.   *The generally-held idea that intelligence declines with old age*
c.   *The claim that emotional intelligence is more important than 'hard' intelligence*
d.   *Calls for more research into the effects of ageing on mental ability*

(IELTS exam, sample academic reading, multiple choice)

What does it mean?

Support is used figuratively in academic language to describe arguments or evidence which strengthen an opinion, claim, argument, or theory.

More loosely, **support** can also mean simply that somebody is a supporter of an idea or cause - in the same way that a football supporter **supports** a particular team.

How to answer:

Writers B and C support writer A's claim (writer B gives a specific example to illustrate how emotional intelligence is more important than 'hard' intelligence, while writer C uses a metaphor to make a similar point).

The correct answer is (d) Jackie Bride is quoted by the writer to support calls for more research into the effects of ageing on mental ability (she questions why so little money is invested into researching a health issue that is set to become an epidemic within the next twenty years, and the writer develops this argument in the paragraph immediately following).

Other discursive constructions

- *Rawlinson's theory is provocative and, on the surface at least, even compelling. However, the key premises are little more than assumptions, **unsupported** by hard evidence.*
- *Were Rawlinson's assumptions **supported** by hard evidence, his provocative theory might be said to be truly compelling.*
- *It should be stressed that Rawlinson's otherwise compelling theory is **supported** by little more than assumption and provocative speculation.*
- *Rawlinson's provocative theory, while lacking hard evidence, is nevertheless **supported** by a number of other experts in the field.*

Be careful!

1. When the word **support** is used in an academic context, it usually collocates with (or implies) '*theory*', '*idea*', or some other claim to fact. However, in other contexts, **support** has other meanings, for example:

'*While he was unable to work, his wife **supported** him*' (financially)
'*After his mother died, his friend stayed with him to **support** her*' (emotionally)
'*She **supports** the new cross-party movement*' (political)

2. **Support** can also be used in a similar way as a noun:

'*The council's plan for a new business centre was scrapped due to a lack of public **support**.*'

'*The new research might lend **support** to Rawlinson's provocative theory.*'

UNIT 6 TEST!

Below is a sample CAE essay task and a sample essay answer with keywords removed. Fill in the spaces in the essay with the keywords from Unit 6.

Your college class has been invited by a large international company to identify the main reasons why talented individuals leave the company and what the best methods are for encouraging staff retention. Following a visit to the company with your class and a meeting with some of the employees, you have made the notes below:

Main reasons staff leave the company
- Better pay offered elsewhere
- Lack of travel/international work placements
- Hours too inflexible

Best methods for making staff stay
- More pay for less popular shifts
- Offer overseas experience
- Home office option

Some opinions expressed in the meeting

"Other companies pay double or triple for weekend work."
"I like this company, but I worry that long-term, my options will be limited if I don't get experience working in a foreign country early on in my career."
"It's not just about money: I think the company needs to do more to recognise the importance of family life and responsibilities."

TASK: *Write an essay for your tutor discussing TWO of the reasons why staff leave the company, and TWO of the methods for encouraging them to stay. You should then **suggest which is the most important reason and which is the most important method** for the company to consider, **giving reasons** to support your choices.*

You may, if you wish, make use of the opinions expressed in the meeting but you should use your own words as far as possible.
*Write your answer in **220-260** words*

How to best address staff retention issues

This essay is (1)_____ with staff retention and specifically, the main factors behind staff turnover and how these might best be addressed in a way that improves outcomes for both employees and the company.

Firstly, from the meeting we conducted with employees, what is clear is that much of the outflow of personnel can be (2)_____ to a perception that other companies pay more for equivalent roles. A survey of similar companies' remuneration packages suggests these claims are generally (3)_____ but it must be (4)_____ that the issue of workers' pay should not be viewed in isolation, but rather in direct relation to shift patterns and options for more flexible working – especially (5)_____ that many employees will want to start families at some point in their careers.

Correspondingly, this analysis is (6)_____ by workers' own comments, which singled out weekend work and inflexible working hours as key areas of dissatisfaction. Further consultation (7)_____ that the two most effective responses to these issues would be to introduce bonuses for weekend work and an option for home office.

If we (8)_____ that these measures will be successful in improving staff retention, then the significant savings in recruitment and training and related efficiency savings should be sufficient to offset the increased cost of paying workers a premium for weekend work.

(9)_____ the initial difficulties involved in implementing a workable home office arrangement, it would seem logical to begin first with an immediate pay increase for weekend work. Furthermore, pay is also (10)_____ with approval and praise. Ultimately, it comes down to job satisfaction and the feeling of being valued.

(267 words)

Congratulations! You've completed 60% of your essential exam vocabulary revision for the C1 exam!

UNIT 7: FUNCTIONAL SPEECH VERBS

Functional speech verbs are words which describe a reason for speaking. They are important for the C1 exam student for three reasons:

1. They are often used in exam questions, and in writing exam tasks to tell you what you should do in order to pass.
2. They should be understood in terms of <u>function</u> and <u>functional exponent</u> (explanation below).
3. They are also reported speech verbs. Using a variety of reported speech verbs is one way of increasing your vocabulary range and raising your grammar level, and is often recommended on creative writing courses for native speakers.

To explain in more detail, let's take the first keyword from this unit: **Advise.**

Firstly, it's a typical functional speech verb you would expect to find in an exam question like *'What phrase does Colin use to **advise** Jake in paragraph one?'* Similarly, it is often used in instructions for writing a letter or essay *'...give your* *opinion about your friend's problem and* **advise** *him/her about the possible options'*.

Secondly, you should understand the word in terms of function and functional exponent. The <u>function</u> connected to the verb **Advise** is *'to give advice'*, meaning *'to provide beneficial information, suggestions, or opinions, especially related to a particular problem, situation or challenge'*. The <u>functional exponent</u> is any special word or phrase which is used to signify or express this function. There are usually several options; a typical exponent for the function of giving advice is *'If I were you...'* Clearly, this is important if the question asks you to identify the special phrase a speaker or writer uses to give advice, or if an essay task asks you to give advice: you need to know and use the related exponents.

Thirdly, in C1 level writing and speech you need to avoid repetitions of *'I said/he said/she said'*, or even worse *'I was like:/he was like:/she was like: OMG!'* Of course, in real life, people do often speak like this in fluent, informal conversation, but the C1 exam is not quite the same as real life and in the exam, you have a relatively short space and time in which to show off your higher level language. A well-placed sentence using reported speech with an appropriate reported speech verb (*the doctor advised me to take rest and drink plenty of water*) will help you gain higher marks.

In this unit, ten functional speech verbs are presented with reference to how they may be used in exam questions or essay tasks, their function and functional exponents, and how they should be used in reported speech.

1. Advise

Example:

*What phrase does Colin use to **advise** Jake in paragraph one?*

-----

*In your reply to Claire's email, you should give your opinion about her problem and **advise** her about the possible options.*

What does it mean?

The <u>function</u> of the verb **advise** is '*to give advice*', meaning '*to provide beneficial information or opinion, especially related to a particular problem, situation or challenge*'.

<u>Functional exponents</u> include:

'If I were you, I would....'
'In my opinion...'
'Perhaps the best thing for you to do is...'
'You should...'
'If I can give you some advice...'
'As your friend/doctor/teacher, I would advise...'
'Wouldn't it be sensible to...?

How to answer:

Colin uses the phrase 'wouldn't it be sensible to...?' to advise Jake to prepare a presentation for his interview.

----

*...I do think, Claire, that your argument with your mother is probably a storm in a teacup and once you have both had a chance to calm down **you should** call her and quickly suggest a walk in the park or a meeting for a coffee - then you can chat together in a neutral environment and hopefully move on.*

<u>How to use **advise** in reported speech:</u>

*I **advised Claire** to allow some time and then call her mother to invite her for a coffee and a chat.*

Be careful!

1. Don't confuse the verb **advise** (spelled with an 's' and pronounced with a 'z') and the noun 'advice' (spelled with a 'c' and pronounced with an 's')
2. Many exponents for giving advice such as 'in my opinion' and 'I think' are also used for giving opinions. Opinions and advice are closely related and sometimes the same - but not always!

2. Admit *and* Deny

Example:

*Why do you think Betty refuses to **admit** to spraying the graffiti?*

----

*What phrase does Betty use to **deny** the police officer's accusation?*

What does it mean?

The <u>function</u> of the verb **to admit** is to accept a claim made about you, or a claim that you are responsible for a crime or misdemeanor.

The <u>function</u> of the verb **to deny** is to argue against a claim made about you, or a claim that you are responsible for a crime or misdemeanor.

<u>Functional exponents</u> for and phrases associated with **admit** include:

'I admit (that)…'
'I accept (that)…'
'It was me'
'You've got me'
'Okay, fair enough'

<u>Functional exponents</u> for and phrases associated with **deny** include:

'It wasn't me'

'I don't accept that'
'It's got nothing to do with me'
'I don't know anything about that'
'You're barking up the wrong tree'

How to answer:

*Betty **denies** spraying the graffiti not so much because of the risk of official punishment but rather because she doesn't want her mother to find out.*

Betty uses the phrase 'it's got nothing to do with me' to deny the police officer's accusation.

How to use **admit** in reported speech:

*Betty **refused to admit to spraying** the graffiti/ Betty **refused to admit that she had sprayed** the graffiti.*

How to use **deny** in reported speech:

*Betty **denied spraying** the graffiti/Betty **denied she had sprayed** the graffiti.*

Be careful!

1. **Admit** and **Deny** are favourite words in the C1 exam and you should make sure you know what they mean and how they are used.
2. **Admit** and **Deny** also have another meaning, *'to accept guests'* and *'to refuse entry/permission'*
3. **Admit** is also used in the phrase *'to admit defeat'* meaning, *'to accept you have lost (a game/competition/battle)'*.

3. Argue

Example:

*How does Maxine **argue** her point against that of her teacher?*

Argue *either FOR or AGAINST the proposal for the changes to the college timetable.*

What does it mean?

In an academic context, the <u>function</u> of the verb **to argue** is 'to defend your theory or opinion, ideally using fact-based evidence and logic. Classical rhetoric also includes appeals to 'ethos' (personal character and reputation) and 'pathos' (passion and emotion).

Similarly, the noun **argument,** in an academic context, refers to the way a person defends their theory or opinion, in an academic or practical, constructive context.

<u>Functional exponents</u> include:

'I would argue that...'
'Based on the evidence...'
'Based on the logic...'
'Allow me to explain...'
'According to the experts/ the mathematical model/ this person who was present at the time...'
'In my experience...'
'It is my position that..'

How to answer:

Maxine questions the motivation behind the proposed changes, suggesting that profit is being placed before quality.

---

*...**It is my position that** the proposed changes to the college timetable are ill-thought through in respect of students who live off campus and part-time students, many of whom are mature students with young children. Furthermore, it appears the changes are driven by a cost-cutting agenda rather than any goal to improve quality of education or student experience. Given that the college has posted record profits this year, should it be necessary to compromise teaching quality and student attainment simply for the sake of lining pockets?*

<u>How to use **argue** in reported speech:</u>

*Maxine **argued** against the proposed changes.*

*Maxine **argued** that the proposed changes **were** ill-thought through and prioritised profit over performance.*

Be careful!

Learners often confuse the formal and informal meanings of **'argue'** and 'argument'.

Outside of an academic/logical context, **'argue'** and 'argument' are more likely to mean 'personal disagreement' or 'fight'. When a couple *'have an argument'*, it is possible that they will use logic - but it is also possible they will shout or throw things..!

Accordingly, you have to be very careful to consider the exact context when deciding what sort of argument is being referred to. *'Maxine argues with her teacher'* could mean an intelligent debate, it could mean a fight, or it could be something in-between ...we need more context to decide. However, *'Maxine argues her point against that of her teacher'* is more specific and suggests a rational, logical argument rather than an explosive outburst.

4. Caution (against)

Example:

What phrase does Jack's uncle use to caution against making a rash decision?

In your reply to Jack's email, suggest why Jack's uncle may have cautioned him.

What does it mean?

The <u>function</u> of the verb **to caution** is to *warn* somebody of a possible danger, difficulty, or penalty.

<u>Functional exponents and phrases include:</u>

If I were you...
Perhaps/Maybe/It might be

Careful/ Be careful
Think carefully
Hey!/ Wait!/ Stop!

How to answer:

Jack's uncle cautions against 'jumping the gun' in asking for a promotion too soon after getting the job.

...It's true that things were different when your uncle was working for a big company: everything happens faster these days, as you say. All the same, I'm sure he is just looking out for your best interests rather than simply trying to prove a point or interfere. Generally, I think it's good to have his experienced advice, even if you choose not to follow it in every situation.

How to use **caution (against)** in reported speech:

*Jack's uncle **cautioned against** jumping the gun.*
*Jack's uncle **cautioned him against** jumping the gun.*
*Jack's uncle **cautioned him not to** jump the gun.*

Be careful!

1. The verb **to caution** is most often used with **against** to stress the meaning of cautionary *advice* - more typically an 'informal' warning not to do something.
2. Used without **against**, the verb **to caution** often means a formal warning - for example, from a soldier, or officer of the law:

    *'The partisan was **cautioned to** surrender.'*
    *'The police officer **cautioned** the youngsters.'*
    'The youngsters were given a formal <u>caution</u> by the police officer.' (<u>noun form</u>)

3. The related noun *'precaution'* refers to a preventative measure taken in advance to minimise risk, even if the risk is small - for example:

    'Although bears were uncommon in the area, we took the usual <u>precaution</u> of not keeping any food inside our tent at night.'

5. Claim

Example:

*What does the second speaker **claim** in response to the first speakers question?*

---

*In your book review, say whether you think the writer **claims** too much or if the writer's claims are reasonable and justified.*

What does it mean?

There are two main <u>functions</u> of the verb **to claim**:

1. (In academic argument) to say a particular thing - often a personal theory - is true, or has a special property, even if there is no hard evidence, or if there is conflicting evidence.

<u>Functional exponents</u> and phrases include:

It is my firm belief that…
I hold that…
It's like this:
The truth is…
I'm prepared to go on the record to say that...

2. (In legal language) to take ownership of something, or to argue that something legally belongs to you.
<u>Functional exponents</u> and phrases include:

I assert my right/claim over…
This belongs to me
I am the legal owner of…

How to answer:

*The second speaker **claims** that human civilisation is far older than previously assumed.*

Having read key sections of the book, I have to say that the writer's headline-grabbing claims are just that: a marketing ploy intended to drive book sales. In the book itself, the writer takes a far more cautious tone, using evasive language to steer around the thornier issues. The book does raise some important and timely questions - it's just a pity the author doesn't have the courage to tackle them

How to use **claim** in reported speech:

*The writer **claimed** that human civilisation was far older than previously assumed.*

*The writer **had claimed** that human civilisation was far older than previously assumed, but when I read her book, I was not able to identify her position on this key point that was so central to the marketing campaign.*

Be careful!

1. There are several synonyms of the verb **to claim**, which use the noun form '*claim*':

Make a claim
Stake a claim
Put forward a claim

2. There are also various collocations which use the verb form (**to claim** + noun):

Claim your innocence
Claim sanctuary
Claim responsibility

6. Counter

Example:

*How does Henry **counter** his classmate's point about the bus?*
---
*...In your essay, you should **counter** any arguments against your chosen option.*

What does it mean?

The <u>function</u> of the verb **to counter** is to directly disagree with somebody else's point, by either identifying a flaw in their argument, or suggesting a better alternative.

<u>Functional exponents and phrases include:</u>

My objection is…
I'd like to pick up that point if I may…
The problem with that is…
Yes, but…
Wouldn't it be better to…?
Isn't it rather that…?
Isn't it fairer to say…?
Only if…
In your experience perhaps, but…
As a matter of fact…

How to answer:

*Henry **counters** his classmate's claim about the comparative practicality of the bus by pointing out that the hotel is only a few minutes walk from the railway station, thereby negating any practical advantage the bus might have had over the train.*

…Given that the hotel is within easy walking distance of the railway station, there is no comparative advantage to hiring a bus for the trip, especially as the journey by train is more direct, faster, and arguably more comfortable.

<u>How to use **counter** in reported speech:</u>

*Henry **countered** his classmate's point about the bus.*

Be careful!

1. The verb **to counter** always describes a response/reaction. In this way, **counter** has a more specific meaning than **argue**.

7. Conclude

Example:

What does Ben **conclude** *as a result of his manager's answer?*

What phrase does the manager use to **conclude** *the formal part of the meeting?*

...You should **conclude** *your report with your recommendation of ONE of the options.*

What does it mean?

There are two main <u>functions</u> of the verb **to conclude**:

1. To form an opinion or make a judgement or assessment, often through inductive reasoning. <u>Functional exponents</u> include:

    Then...
    In that case...
    I will assume that...
    It seems...
    It appears...

2. To formally end an essay, discussion, or meeting. <u>Functional exponents</u> include:

    To conclude...
    In conclusion...
    Finally...
    Ultimately...
    To bring matters to a close...

How to answer:

In response to his manager's answer, Ben **concludes** *that updating the company software will have to wait another year.*

The manager uses the phrase 'moving on to less important matters...' to signal the conclusion of the formal part of the meeting.

...In conclusion, I firmly recommend a renovation of the old building rather than its demolition and replacement, for the reasons outlined above.

How to use **conclude** in reported speech:

*Ben **concluded that** updating the company software would have to wait.*

Be careful!

1. ***Concluded (that)*** can be a reported speech construction which refers in speech to a conclusion, or alternatively it can refer to a mental (unspoken) conclusion:

*Ben privately **concluded (that)** his boss was crazy.*

2. ***Concluded with*** + noun / *conclude by* + **Ving** are constructions which refer to 'formal endings' and do not necessarily constitute 'reported speech' in the technical sense:

*He **concluded** the wedding speech **with** a toast.*
*He **concluded** by toasting the happy couple.*

8. Concur

Example:

*What point made by person A is **concurred with** by two other people?*

---

*In your essay, decide if your views **concur with** those of the panel.*

What does it mean?

The <u>function</u> of the verb **to concur** is to agree formally with a point in an academic or diplomatic discussion or debate.

<u>Functional exponents</u> and phrases include:

I agree
I am in agreement
Our positions are in line
That position reflects my own
I think we share the same perspective

How to answer:

*Persons C and D **concur with** Person A's point that truly settling in a foreign country takes at least five years.*

---

*I **concur** that blame for the accident rests mainly with the building company and that suitable compensation should be paid to the claimant. In that respect, our positions are in line. However, the amount of compensation should reflect the fact that the claimant made a personal decision not to use safety equipment that the building company had provided for the purpose of limiting the severity of any injury.*

How to use **concur** in reported speech:

*The lawyer **concurred** - albeit with certain caveats - that blame for the accident rested mainly with the building company.*

Be careful!

1. **Concur** is a highly formal synonym for '*agree*', and should only be used in formal academic, legal, or diplomatic contexts.
2. Confusingly, the adjective '*concurrent*' and adverb '*concurrently*', have a different meaning: '*at the same time*'.

9. Speculate

Example:

*What phrase in paragraph 3 does Andrew use to make clear he is **speculating** rather than asserting a strong opinion?*

---

*In your letter, you should **speculate** as to why fewer people than anticipated have applied to join the course.*

What does it mean?

The <u>function</u> of the verb **to speculate** is *'to guess'*, or *'to provide an assessment, explanation, or prediction'*, based on the immediate evidence available.

<u>Functional exponents include:</u>

I think
Maybe
Perhaps
Possibly
It seems to me
It might be that
If I were to speculate, I would say that

How to answer:

Andrew uses the phrase 'it might be that' to indicate that his assessment is purely speculative and not intended to represent a considered opinion or solid position on his part.

...It might be that the low enrolment numbers for this course may be connected to a slowness in embracing online marketing as the best means of targeting school-leavers. This possibility should at least be explored.

<u>How to use **speculate** in reported speech:</u>

*Andrew **speculated** that the low enrolment numbers <u>were</u> related to marketing strategy.*

Be careful!

1. **Speculate** is a key 'teaching word' in the teaching of 'English as a Foreign Language', especially in the Cambridge courses and exams. 'Speculating language' is a classroom-term used for the kind of functional exponents listed above.

2. The other meaning of the verb **to speculate** is that of '*financial speculation*', synonymous with the verb '*to invest*', especially through a third party or via the open market. The noun person is '*speculator*', which always has the financial meaning of 'investor' or 'trader', usually on the open market (stocks, shares, currency, etc.).

10. State

Example:

*In Paragraph 1, what key requirement is **stated** in the information provided to prospective tenants?*

---

*In your letter, **state** your position on the proposed statue and suggest how people on both sides of the debate might be satisfied.*

What does it mean?

The function of the verb **to state** is to make a statement of truth: either a claim to a fact, or a firm opinion. Informally, to **state** something is to say something casually in a 'matter of fact' kind of way. Formally, to **state** something is to declare something to be true, or to clearly outline your opinion or position. Often, *statements* are by their nature very simple and require no special phrases or exponents. However, some exponents are listed immediately below.

Functional exponents include:

My opinion is that...
It is my position that...

It is my view that..
For the record…
Let it be noted that…

How to answer:

In paragraph one, **it is stated** *that all tenants must be over the age of 25, or be prepared to pay for a full year's rent in advance.*

…Personally, I don't have a preference for either a traditional or a modern style as long as the final result is tasteful, appropriate to the writer whom it commemorates, and sensitive to the surrounding architecture, which I am told is neither especially old nor über-modern. If feelings are so divided, why not also divide the funding and commission two statues to represent the old and the new?

How to use **state** in reported speech:

The contributor **stated** *his indifference to the style of the proposed statue.*

Be careful!

1. The noun form *'statement'* is commonly used to describe an official declaration, either to be formally recorded as part of a legal process, or announced publicly:

    The witness gave a statement at the police station
    The defendant's lawyer made a statement outside the court
    A government aide issued a statement to the press.

2. The phrase 'to make a statement' also has a figurative meaning, 'behave or act in an impressive or provocative way, calculated to have an obvious effect, usually to impress:

I think he wore the Hawaiian shirt to the office to make a statement.

The foreign delegate made a statement by arriving with a huge entourage of celebrities and security staff.

UNIT 7 TEST!

Fill in the gaps using the ten keywords from this unit - some words can be used in more than one place!

1. The two scientists have very different opinions but on this one point they do _____.

2. After a long day, the panel _____ that a lack of evidence meant that no further action would be taken.

3. Lisa won the debate after successfully _____ that her proposal was the most adventurous.

4. Alternative history novels make interesting reading for those who enjoy _____ about how events might have turned out differently.

5. Those travelling abroad are _____ to take out travel insurance.

6. At the border, I was asked to _____ my name and address, and my reason for visiting the country.

7. Finally, my little brother _____ that he had eaten all the chocolate biscuits.

8. Having been accused of pedantry, Alex _____ that it was a lazy approach to detail that had been the main reason for the problem in the first place.

9. New students were _____ against walking alone at night.

10. The company _____ its new drug can greatly reduce the symptoms of travel sickness.

Answers: 1. *concur* 2. *concluded* 3. *arguing* 4. *speculating* 5. *advised* 6. *state* 7. *admitted* 8. *countered* 9. *cautioned/advised* 10. *claims/argues*

Congratulations! You've completed 70% of your essential exam vocabulary revision for the C1 exam!

UNIT 8: FEELINGS (VERB-3 ADJECTIVES)

'Feeling words' represent one of the 'must-revise' vocabulary topics for anyone preparing for a language exam. These adjectives and related parts of speech are likely to feature in all parts of the exam (reading, writing, speaking, listening) and they are favourite words for examiners.

At B2 intermediate level, students are already expected to know and use a wide range of 'feeling' words, including but not limited to: *happy, sad, tired, tiring, fresh, excited, exciting, bored, boring, proud, relaxed, relaxing, interested, interesting, frightened, frightening, confused, confusing, frustrated, frustrating, disappointed, disappointing, embarrassed, embarrassing, and jealous.*

You will notice that many of these feeling words are also verbs which can be used in the V3 passive *-ed* form to describe a feeling (for example, *I was tired*) or in the V-ing active form to describe the thing that causes the feeling (*the journey was tiring*). The verb itself can also be used to create a sentence with a similar meaning (*these journeys tire me*). This versatility makes verb-adjectives very useful in the exam.

This unit focuses on ten slightly-less common verb-adjectives that are very useful for the exam at C1 level.

For each verb-adjective, the *-ed* and the *-ing* form are given, as well as the basic verb. Synonyms, antonyms, noun forms and important collocations (typical combinations with other words) are also listed.

1. Amused

Example:

*Why is Gabriella **amused**?*
*What **amuses** Gabriella?*
*What does Gabriella find **amusing**?*
*What is the source of Gabriella's **amusement**?*

What does it mean?

Amused is most often used to describe someone who is smiling or laughing at something unusual or mildly comic.

<u>Synonyms</u> include *tickled* and *entertained.*
<u>Antonyms</u> include *serious, sober,* and *bored.* The negative **unamused** is only normally used in an ironic or understated way.
The <u>noun form</u> is **amusement**. The <u>verb form</u> is **to amuse**.

The word **amused** comes from the word *muse* from ancient Greek mythology. The *muses* were divine creatures said to captivate and inspire poets and artists with their beauty and divine quality. This original meaning *'to fix your attention on something', 'to gaze in wonder on something', 'to be curious about something', 'to be idly entertained'* is still sometimes used:

The youths spent their money at the <u>amusement arcade</u> (gaming hall)
The children <u>amused themselves</u> with simple toys.

How to answer:

*Gabriella is **amused** by the high-pitched voice of the tour guide.*

Be careful!

The feeling adjective **amused** is very important because there are very few direct synonyms in English to describe feeling this way. Because of this, English speakers will often use verb phrases or idioms like '*He found it hilarious*' or '*They were in stitches*', or '*She laughed her head off*'.

2. Challenged

Example:

*Some psychologists have criticised a 'helicopter parenting' style which prevents children from ever feeling **challenged**. What kind of problems can this cause for children as they grow up?*

---

*Why are **challenging** experiences important in a child's upbringing?*

What does it mean?

A challenge is a test - usually not an exam but an informal test presented by life. To feel **challenged** is to feel tested in your current situation. A crucial part of this feeling is the sense of the unknown and the experience of using your personal initiative and instinct, as well as your knowledge and skills, in order to survive the test, or even to excel. The other crucial part of the concept of challenge is that, win or lose, challenge can be educational and satisfying. It's the reason sports and puzzles are so popular. Challenges can be tough and even deeply unpleasant, but life without challenge is dull.

This means **challenged** can refer to a negative feeling, a positive feeling, or it can be positive and negative at the same time. Often, it is used in a positive way, in line with the general opinion that an element of challenge is important - even essential - for health and success.

<u>Synonyms</u> include: *tested, trialled, under pressure*
<u>Antonyms</u> include: *bored, insulated, inexperienced.* The negative **unchallenged** is used to mean 'unfulfilled', 'bored'.
The <u>noun form</u> is **challenge** (*the job lacked challenge*) The <u>verb form</u> is also **to challenge** (see Be Careful!)

How to answer:

Parenting is always a controversial topic but there should be no doubt that overprotectiveness, while perhaps understandable from the point of view of a worried parent, is ultimately counterproductive. 'Helicopter parenting' as it is known, or the practice of sweeping all problems from a child's path and micromanaging their every day, prevents children from developing practical problem solving skills and learning how to manage risk, stress, and failure, rendering them unable to look after themselves and therefore more prone to accidents and depression.

Be careful!

Challenged has a special meaning as a verb in a legal/political/academic/debating context:

*The panel's first ruling was successfully **challenged** by an action group and now the case has been passed to a higher authority for further consideration.*

A *legal challenge* is a formal disagreement backed up by strong argument. This meaning is related to the noun-person **challenger** - somebody who *issues a challenge*, traditionally one-on-one combat.

3. Daunted

Example:

*What reason is given in the text for Melissa feeling **daunted** by the prospect of beginning university?*

What reason is provided in the text to explain why Melissa considered beginning university to be such a daunting prospect?

What does it mean?

To feel **daunted** is to feel impressed by the scale, difficulty, or significance of a challenge or responsibility. It is not the same as feeling worried or scared, although a *'daunting challenge'* is certainly one that makes you feel 'how am I ever going to do *that*', and might well make you feel worried or scared also.

Synonyms include: *intimidated, overawed, disconcerted*
Antonyms include: *confident, unfazed, undaunted*
The verb form is **to daunt.** There is no obvious or well-used noun form for C1 purposes.

How to answer:

*According to the text, Melissa is **daunted** by the prospect of beginning university mainly because she has never lived away from her childhood home before.*

Be careful!

Daunted and **daunting** are favourite words in the C1 exam - clearly examiners feel that this is a perfect example of C1 level vocabulary. Try to use this word to talk about very big, life-changing challenges and you will help to convince the examiner that you have a C1 level vocabulary.

4. Exhilarated

Example:

What does Richard mean when he says that he expects a holiday to leave him feeling **exhilarated** *rather than just excited?*

What does Richard mean when he says he prefers **exhilarating** *holidays to those which are merely exciting?*

What does it mean?

Originally, **exhilarated** meant '*cheerful*', '*excited*' or '*animated*', as you might describe a person having a good time at a party, telling jokes and laughing. Nowadays however, **exhilarated** usually means '*thrilled*' or '*stimulated*', usually as a result of a high-octane sport like snowboarding or Formula 1 racing, or skydiving. More figuratively, **exhilarating** may also describe bold, meaty discussion, or a refreshingly different cultural experience.

Synonyms include: *thrilled, stimulated, invigorated.*
Antonyms incude: *bored, stagnant, lethargic. Unexhilarated is* not a word.
The noun form is **exhilaration.** The verb form is **to exhilarate.**

How to answer:

According to Richard, excitement is more of an everyday feeling and is often about 'looking forward to something', like a child excited in the week before Christmas. **Exhilaration**, *on the other hand, refers to a full sensual and psychological stimulation which 'blows out all the cobwebs' and leaves you feeling renewed and vital.*

Be Careful!

Exhilarated and **exhilarating** are used fairly often in the C1 exam. Be aware that the meaning has changed over time (see above) so in some older texts the older meaning may still apply.

5. Enlightened

Example:

*When Berta says she feels **enlightened** she means*

a. *She feels she has a more accurate understanding of something*
b. *She feels a weight off her shoulders*
c. *She feels she has a completely new understanding of something*
d. *She feels more clever than other people*

What does it mean?

Light allows us to see while darkness conceals the unknown. For this reason, light is an ancient metaphor for knowledge, especially rational knowledge. To **enlighten** somebody is therefore to supply him or her with knowledge about something. To feel **enlightened** in this way is to 'feel like your eyes are opened for the first time'. In the epic sense, **enlightenment** is a revelation - a paradigm shift, revolutionary discovery, or a religious conversion.

Confusingly, there are other, slightly different meanings:

1. The simple everyday discovery of new information (often ironic or sarcastic):

    *Do please **enlighten** us as to what your plan was for finding a hotel during the busiest week of the year.*

2. As a synonym for 'educated/progressive' as opposed to 'uneducated/backward/repressed':

    *New evidence suggests that the Victorians were far more sexually **enlightened** than was previously thought.*

Synonyms include: *illuminated, apprised, worldly*
Antonyms include: *dim, backward, repressed*
The noun form is **enlightenment**. The *Enlightenment* in history is spelled with a capital E. The verb form is **to enlighten**.

How to answer:

The answer could be (a), (c) , or (d), depending on the context. The basic answer, without context, would be (c).

Be careful!

Don't confuse with *'lighten'* which can mean either to make something less heavy, or to make something - for example a room or colour - less dark. **Enlighten** always refers to knowledge or new information.

6. Inspired

Example:

Describe an event or story which has made you feel inspired.
*Describe an **inspiring** event or story.*

---

*Describe someone in your life who has given you **inspiration**.*
*Describe someone in your life who has **inspired** you.*

What does it mean?

To feel **inspired** is to feel positive, creative, optimistic, or emotionally moved as a result of a specific positive experience or influence.

Inspiration may come from the beauty of nature (often called Romantic inspiration). Frequently, inspiration is the result of witnessing the achievement or good example of another person, or it may be the creative reaction to a challenge or problem.

Inspiring stories often involve groups or individuals succeeding against great challenge and hardship, or achieving remarkable things with little help or support, or simply staying positive and happy in the face of great suffering.

Inspired may be just a feeling, or it may describe creative motivation when used in the passive with the infinitive:

*After seeing the poor boy's home-made bicycle, the engineering graduate **was inspired to create** a bicycle that could be produced easily from recycled materials.*

(was inspired to create = Vtobe + V3passive + infinitive)

<u>Synonyms</u> include: *moved, impressed, galvanised*
<u>Antonyms</u> include: *depressed, disillusioned, uninspired*
The <u>noun form</u> is **inspiration**. The <u>verb form</u> is **to inspire**

How to answer:

*I recently watched a film about an innocent man who escaped from prison. Even though he had to suffer for many years, he never lost his sense of pride and hope and inner strength and I found this **inspiring**. I think we can all use this inner strength.*
---
*I think my sister has always been a good role model to me because she has always been very confident about getting out in the world. She went travelling on her own for a whole year and kept in touch with me the whole time and as result I grew up believing the same was possible for me - that I could be brave and adventurous too. I definitely took **inspiration** from her when it came to applying for a job in America.*

Be careful!

1. Talking about people or things that give you inspiration is a common question in the speaking part of the exam, so it's a good idea to ask yourself now: what things and which people have inspired you and why? How did these things or people change your life?

2. **Inspired** and **inspiring** collocate with the word 'performance' and other performance-related nouns. An **inspired performance** means that the performer is inspired by the gods of art or sport, and performing at the peak of his or her ability, delivering something truly special. An **inspiring performance** means that the audience is inspired by the performance.

7. Intrigued

Example:

Why does Alice feel **intrigued** *by the sign on the door?*

What is **intriguing** *about the sign on the door?*

What does it mean?

To feel **intrigued** is to feel curious about something unusual or mysterious, with the result that you want to find out more.

Narrative intrigue is a fundamental principle of drama and storytelling: in thrillers and dramas especially, **intrigue**, or the unanswered question, is what keeps the audience following the story - the audience wants to know *why, how, and who?*

Intrigued can also be used as a synonym for 'fascinated'

Synonyms include: *curious, fascinated, captivated*
Antonyms include: *bored, unaffected, uninterested*
The noun form is **intrigue**, the verb form is also **to intrigue**

How to answer:

Alice is **intrigued** *by the cryptic, counter-intuitive message "knock if you don't want to enter".*

Be careful!

Intrigue also has a second, Machiavellian meaning, using the verb or the noun. This type of intrigue will often describe a secret plot, especially in the context of power and politics:

The Tudor dynasty and its various **intrigues** *provide much interest for historians and writers of historical fiction.*

8. Misled

Example:

*Why did John feel **misled** by the ticket sellers?*

---

*What was **misleading** in the way the tickets were sold?*

What does it mean?

To feel **misled** is to feel tricked into believing something that isn't true, or doing something wrong against better judgement.

Misleading information may be deliberately clever language, selective information or simply carelessness - in all cases, it 'leads' people to the wrong conclusion without necessarily 'lying'.

<u>Synonyms</u> include: *misinformed, tricked, duped.*
<u>Antonyms</u> include: *well-informed, well-treated, aided.*
There is no noun form. The <u>verb form</u> is **to mislead.**

Be careful!

1. The verb 2 and 3 forms of the verb 'to lead' are irregular (led). This explains why the V3 adjective is spelled **misled** while the Verb 1 and V-ing forms are **mislead** and **misleading.**
2. Literally, *to lead* means to '*show the way*' or '*be the leader*'. **Mislead** is always used figuratively in the negative sense.
3. The other meaning of **misled** is to be negatively influenced - especially into a life of crime:

    *"The judge accepted that the young thief had fallen into bad company and had been **misled** and exploited by people he had looked up to as role models".*

4. Related to (3.) is the adjective-phrase **easily-led** meaning *impressionable, gullible, vulnerable to exploitation.*
5. **Poorly-led** refers to a group of soldiers or employees who have a bad leader (**well-led** is the opposite).

9. Overwhelmed

Example:

What does Jack mean when he says the first week at university left him feeling **overwhelmed**?

What does Jack mean when he says the first week at university was **overwhelming**?

a. *He was barely able to stay in control of everything*
b. *He was made to feel very welcome*
c. *He missed home*
d. *He was disappointed*

What does it mean?

Overwhelmed literally means to be drowned, especially by floodwater. The word is often used figuratively to mean 'defeated' or 'shocked'. To feel **overwhelmed** emotionally is to feel shocked or under pressure as a result of sheer amount of strong emotion, work, stress, multiple responsibilities, new information, and so on.

Synonyms include: *overcome, dazed, shocked.*
Antonyms include: *unaffected, unruffled, unmoved.* The negative **underwhelmed** is used ironically to mean '*unimpressed*'.
There is no noun form. The verb form is **to underwhelm.**

How to answer:

The answer is (a). Jack found the first week of university **overwhelming** *- the amount of new information and number of new names and faces was too much to take in and Jack felt he was losing his grip.*

Be careful!

Sometimes **overwhelmed** and **overwhelming** are used mainly to add drama and emphasis, with the essential meaning: '*the main impression/feeling was...*'

I was **overwhelmed** *by the generosity of the local people.*

There was an **overwhelming** *sense of relief after the two sides agreed a peace deal.*

10. Threatened

Example:

What does Ian mean when he says he felt **threatened** *by the arrival of a young executive to the company?*

What does it mean?

A threat is a danger or the promise of danger. To be **threatened** means either to receive a **verbal threat** (for example: *"Watch your mouth or I'll watch it for you"*) or to be in existential danger (for example: *Orangutans are a threatened species/logging presents an* **existential threat** *to orangutans*).

To feel **threatened** is to feel in danger, or to feel your position or status is in danger as a result of hostility or competition.

<u>Synonyms</u> include: *insecure, vulnerable, jealous.*
<u>Antonyms</u> include: *invincible, secure, safe.*
The <u>noun form</u> is **threat**. The <u>verb form</u> is to **threaten.**

How to answer:

Ian means that he is worried that the new colleague, if seen as more energetic and having more future potential than Ian, will take Ian's job. Maybe the new colleague has no intention of doing this but still Ian feels insecure in the face of what he regards as younger competition and a **threat** *to his position in the company.*

Be careful!

Don't confuse **threatened** with '*treated*' or '*entreated*'. These are three totally different words with different meanings. **Threat** is also pronounced with an open 'e' while treat and entreat are pronounced with a closed 'i'.

(*To treat* means to behave or act in a certain way towards someone or something or alternatively, to provide a special gift or present. *To entreat* means to attempt to persuade someone or appeal to their reasonable nature).

UNIT 8 TEST!

Fill in the gaps using the ten keywords from this unit - decide whether the *-ed* or *-ing* form should be used to complete each sentence

1. The hotel was advertised in the brochure as having its own private beach but when Helen discovered the beach was actually located 5km away from the hotel, she complained that the information was _____ and demanded her money back.

2. After touring South America, the artist felt _____ to produce a series of paintings depicting South American cultures and folklore.

3. Alone in the boat, surrounded by nothing but ocean as far as the eye could see, Manfred for the first time felt _____ by the challenge ahead of him.

4. Easily bored and able to work well under pressure, Christie always enjoyed _____ projects.

5. At the height of the winter flu epidemic, hospital staff felt _____ by the scale of the crisis.

6. Mark had never really paid any mind to meditation and yoga and healthy eating and all that 'hippy stuff' but after taking part in a mindfulness weekend by chance, he felt truly _____ , as though someone had pulled back a curtain he had never realised was there.

7. The protesters outside the court complained that they felt _____ by what they say was the totally unnecessary presence of security forces in full riot gear, holding snarling dogs.

8. Mary had felt unsure about signing up for the watersports holiday but three days in and she felt _____ by the physical exertion, the fresh air, and the thrill of stepping outside her comfort zone.

9. The foreign guests did not find Melanie's jokes _____. It seemed that her brand of humour did not travel well.

10. At dinner that evening, nobody else seemed bothered by the ambassador's unexplained bandage and newly-acquired limp but Gregory was _____.

Answers: 1. *misleading* 2. *inspired* 3. *daunted/overwhelmed* 4. *challenging* 5. *overwhelmed/daunted* 6. *enlightened* 7. *threatened* 8. *exhilarated* 9. *amusing* 10. *intrigued*

Congratulations! You've completed 80% of your essential exam vocabulary revision for the C1 exam!

UNIT 9: BUSINESS AND FINANCE

'Business English' is considered a specialised vocabulary, as evidenced by the many business English courses and coursebooks on offer. If however, you are preparing for a *general* C1 English exam like IELTS, TOEFL or CAE, you don't need to worry too much about technical business jargon: examiners usually keep technical business language out of the exam.

Nevertheless, as the world of business and finance is so important to daily life, general students of English need to be familiar with some of the more basic business-English keywords that are frequently used in the C1 exam.

1. Credit, debt, interest, *and* mortgages

Example:

*Jim's current account is **in credit** by 200 pounds but he has 2000 pounds **debt** on his **credit card**, on which he pays 50 pounds monthly **interest**. Additionally, he pays 200 pounds each month in **mortgage** repayments. After paying for these and his basic requirements, he has about 200 pounds left each month for leisure, fashion, and holidays. What financial advice would you offer Jim?*

(It's unlikely a real C1 exam question will be so financially focused. However, personal finance is a regular topic!)

What does it mean?

These four words are all linked by the most basic practice of banking: money-lending.

The word **credit** can be confusing because it can refer either to savings (to be **'in credit'**) or it can refer to the ability to borrow money (to **'have credit with/at'**, to be **creditworthy**). A **credit card** allows the user to borrow money from a credit card company.

Debt means money that you have borrowed and must pay back. Technically, any borrowed money is **debt** but the word is most often used in a negative way to describe borrowing that is getting out of control: **bad debt**.

Interest is charged by the lender (the technical word is *levied*) on money that is borrowed, at a percentage agreed by the borrower and the lender. If you have savings, **interest** is paid by the bank to the **creditor** (you) at an agreed percentage.

A **mortgage** is a special type of **loan** (money-lending) made available for the purchase of real estate (a house or apartment, or land with a building project).

How to answer:

Firstly, Jim needs to reduce his monthly spending on non-essentials in order to increase his emergency savings. As a minimum, he should have enough savings to pay three months worth of bills and essentials: As he must pay a minimum of two hundred and fifty pounds each month in **credit card interest** *and* **mortgage repayments,** *he should have savings of seven hundred and fifty pounds plus whatever he needs to pay for food and utilities and other essentials. A thousand pounds is probably a good savings target to aim for and maintain.*

At the same time, Jim needs to start bringing down his **credit card debt** *by paying back more than the minimum interest payment each month. I suspect Jim has buried his head in the sand with this and probably he could even switch to a credit card with a better rate, or even a zero-rate for a fixed period, which might give him enough time to pay off the debt totally. Crucially, Jim needs to make a plan and a monthly budget and make sure he sticks to it. This will mean sacrificing some luxuries for one or two years but then he will be better off and more secure, not to mention free from all that anxiety!*

Be careful!

1. Don't confuse '*lend*' and '*borrow*'. These words are a bit like '*throw*' and '*catch*': The bank *lends* the money *to* the customer; the customer *borrows* the money *from* the bank.
2. **Debt** and **mortgage** are not pronounced the way they are written! The 'b' in **debt** is silent, and the 't' in **mortgage** is silent.
3. **Credit** is related to the word '*credible*' which means '*believable*'. When you are offered **credit**, it means the lender *believes* you can and will pay the money back at a later date.
4. Unpaid credit card **debt** is considered 'bad debt'. Mortgage **debt** is usually considered a good investment, or 'good debt'.

2. Employee *and* Employer

Example:

What are the relative advantages of being an **employee** *compared to being an* **employer***?*

What does it mean?

An **employee** is a worker who is employed by a business or business owner - the **employer**.

English learners often confuse **employee** and **employer**. These are two of the most basic words in everyday life so it's important to get them right at C1 level. Remember that the noun-person 'ee' ending is passive (*employee, interviewee, trainee, mentee*) while the noun person 'r' ending is active (*employer, interviewer, trainer, mentor*).

How to answer:

The key difference between **employee** *and* **employer** *is about the share of risk and profit: the* **employee** *takes little or no share of personal financial risk but at the same time does not share in any company profit. The* **employer** *takes most or all of the risk but also takes most or all of any company profit. Similarly, the* **employee** *also has less responsibility and commitment while the the* **employer** *is tied to a long-term plan and a heavy burden of responsibility.*

Be careful!

Be aware of the related words *employed (in work), unemployed (out of work), employment (world of work/people in work), unemployment (joblessness).* These words are all used regularly in the C1 exam.

3. Entrepreneur

Example:

*'***Entrepreneurs*** need to embrace failure'. To what extent do you agree or disagree with this statement?*

What does it mean?

An **entrepreneur** is somebody who creates a business or 'startup' - in particular, a business that is built on a new idea: a new product or service or an existing product or service with a new twist or application.

How to answer:

Until recently, and especially in Europe and Asia, failure carried a real stigma: business failure was synonymous with 'ruin' and taken as evidence that the failed **entrepreneur** *was unfit for business. By contrast, the American attitude has always been that successive failure is simply part of the road to success - and even a crucial learning experience. Sometimes associated with this culture is the principle of 'failing fast', or being open to quickly identifying and accepting critical flaws in a business plan rather than being too scared to admit them.*

I agree there is certainly something to be learned from this concept - there is definitely nothing to be gained from flogging the proverbial dead horse, so it makes sense to be open to the possibility of failure and to be prepared to abort a doomed project. There is an important difference however, between accepting and celebrating failure: accepting failure and learning how to anticipate and deal with failure is instructive and healthy; inviting failure is not. It seems patently foolish to me to be aiming for failure as a kind of necessary target, even as a staging post in a longer career. As with many debates, I think two extreme positions can be identified here, both of which are unhealthy: the failure-phobic and the failure-fetishist. Clearly the correct approach lies somewhere in-between.

Be careful!

Entrepreneur has a tricky spelling; it's worth practising this spelling a few times. There are also some related words which are even longer: *entrepreneurial* (general adjective), *entrepreneurship* (the personal quality required to be an entrepreneur, especially risk-taking and organisational skills) and *entrepreneurialism* (general/abstract noun).

4. Feedback

Example:

Why do you think customer **feedback** *so important in the development of new products and services?*

What does it mean?

In business, **feedback** means *'review', 'response'* or *'constructive criticism'*.

There are two main types:

1. **Customer/client/user feedback** - the people who use the product or service give their opinions about the product or service.
2. **Personal feedback** - your boss or line manager critically assesses your professional performance, usually as part of a structured professional development program.

How to answer:

*Businesses often use focus groups for testing new products and services in a similar way to pharmaceutical companies conducting controlled trials before making new pharmaceutical products commercially available. Just as new drugs may have unexpected side effects, new products and services often present problems in practice that are not apparent 'on paper'. In addition to testing for functionality (and malfunctions), it is also important to gauge consumer preferences - does the consumer group actually like the product or service and the way it is delivered? Will they buy it? While organising such trials may be costly and time-consuming, targeted **feedback** during the development stage can help companies avoid losing even more money on a 'dud' product or service.*

5. Implementation

Example:

*What problems are usually encountered during the **implementation** of new IT systems in large institutions such as public services like health and education?*

What does it mean?

From the verb *'to implement'* meaning *'to put (something) into practice'*, **implementation** is the noun which refers to the process of introducing a new way of doing something or a new rule or system.

In project management, the **implementation phase** follows the *development phase* or *testing phase,* or the testing phase may be considered part of the implementation phase.

How to answer:

Implementation *of new IT systems in large institutions represents a considerable undertaking, not least because it is usually impossible to fully shut down the operation of the institution, or even accurately predict demand and stress in order to best decide how to stage implementation. This means that implementation invariably takes place in an ad hoc, piecemeal, chaotic fashion over a long period of time, often with parts of the old system running simultaneously with parts of the new system - with inevitable conflicts and problems.*

Added to this is the basic fact that new systems which need to be tailor-made for institutions will almost certainly have bugs which only become evident once the system comes online. Repairing these will involve trial and error and unscheduled system outages. Training the personnel of the institution to use the new system represents another challenge, which may be compounded by workplace-cultural resistance to new ideas and ways of working - especially ways of reporting. Meanwhile, large, bureaucratic management hierarchies typically produce conflicting visions and constraints, and multiple stakeholders from wildly different professions may struggle to communicate with one another effectively during this stressful period.

Finally, there are the hardware and budgetary issues connected to related equipment and infrastructure. These can present extra costs and indecision, all of which may further contribute to slow progress.

Be careful!

Don't confuse the verb **to implement** and the noun **implementation** with the noun '*implement*' meaning 'tool':

Prehistoric man used a variety of **implements** *for making weapons and clothing and preparing food, from flint axes and stone mallets to needles, blades and spoons*

6. (to be) In charge (of something)

Example:

How many people was the CEO ***in charge of****?*
What is Jenny ***in charge of****?*

*Who is **in charge of** enforcing parliamentary rules of debate in the UK House of Commons?*

What does it mean?

To be **in charge of** something is to have power and responsibility in a specific context. A person **in charge** is the leader of a certain group of people, or a person with direct responsibility for something, or the authority in a certain context.

How to answer:

*The CEO, as head of the company, was technically **in charge of** 500 people.*
*Jenny is **in charge of** the accounts department.*
*The House Speaker is **in charge of** enforcing correct procedure and conduct in parliamentary debates in the UK House of Commons.*

Be careful:

1. This phrase is the most common, everyday way of describing official responsibility in English. Make sure you know it!
2. Don't confuse with the other meanings of 'charge': a paid fee (*I paid the parking charge*), a criminal charge (*he was charged with murder*), a stampede (*the elephants/horses/soldiers charged across the field*)

7. Productivity

Example:

*According to the article, what is one way the UK can improve its **productivity**?*

What does it mean?

Productivity in general terms concerns how *productive* a person, company, or country is - that is, how much useful work they can do over a certain period of time.

In business/economic terms, **productivity** is usually measured in currency (for example, dollars, pounds, or Euros). The productivity of a country is usually measured in GDP (Gross domestic product, the total value of goods and services produced in one year) and GDP per Capita (Gross domestic product divided by population).

How to answer:

The writer of the article claims that company investment in more modern and efficient machinery and infrastructure would improve UK **productivity**. *However, the writer admits that this will only happen if government subsidises or otherwise incentivises this investment.*

Be careful!

Use the context to decide whether the general meaning (*I would like to be a writer but I need to work on my* **productivity**) or the technical meaning (**productivity** *issues have hampered company growth*) is being used.

8. Promotion

Example:

What are the possible downsides to getting a **promotion** *at work?*

What are the possible benefits for retailers in holding a **promotion**?

What are the special demands of music **promotion**?

What does it mean?

As the examples above show, there are three different meanings of this word, all related to business.

1. Moving up to a higher level of responsibility at work.

2. A special offer or event designed to increase brand visibility and sell products.
3. Professionally supporting the marketing and commercial development of a product or enterprise.

How to answer:

While **promotion** *to a higher level of responsibility usually comes with higher salary and prestige, it may also involve more work, commitment and stress. Furthermore, not everyone is suited to management roles.*

Retailers often choose to invest in promotions such as 'buy one get one free' offers or schemes which offer consumers 'gifts' in return for tokens or points accrued by spending money in a store. The main objective is either to focus consumers' attention on a new product, to develop consumer loyalty, or to generate a 'buzz' which attracts large numbers of consumers to the store.

Music promoters must be able to see the band or artist as a commercial product while appreciating the delicate human side. They should ideally be well-connected in the music and celebrity industry and be prepared to work long hours, often on the road and late at night.

Be careful!

There is a further, more formal use of the verb *'to promote'* used to mean *'actively encourage'*:

Many headteachers choose to implement a uniform policy in the belief that it **promotes** *a sense of belonging and respect in the schoolchildren.*

9. Soft skills *and* Hard skills

Example:

Do you think it is possible to teach **'soft skills'** *or can they only be learned through experience?*

What does it mean?

Hard skills are things like literacy and numeracy - the ability to read and write and perform mathematical calculations. Hard skills are also things like wood or metal working, or the ability to write software using a particular coding language.

Soft skills include interpersonal and communication skills, charm, good taste, tact, empathy, negotiation, time-management, creativity, free-thinking, creative problem-solving, talent-spotting, leadership and the ability to 'weigh up' a situation or problem.

People frequently disagree on the definition of what does and what doesn't count as a **soft skill**. For example, some people argue that critical analysis is a perfect example of a soft skill while other people feel critical analysis is very standardised and formal, and one of the most basic academic **hard skills**. Also at issue is the term itself: 'soft' arguably suggests 'less important', yet many people argue that these so-called 'soft skills' are actually the most valuable and also the hardest to learn.

How to answer:

The idea that young people can be sent away to an educational institution for several years and return fully equipped to behave properly in polite society and take up leadership roles in politics, law, big business, the church and the military, is not a new one. Indeed, this is the primary aim and 'reason for being' of private education, certainly in the UK.

It is interesting then, that graduates of this system have been consistently identified as being lacking in the key leadership skill of empathy: David Cameron, the former British Prime Minister, and much of his cabinet were private schoolboys educated to be leaders but perhaps these old institutions (Eton, Harrow, Fettes, and so on) are either behind the times or have grown too isolated from mainstream society - or both. It is becoming increasingly fashionable to assert the view that soft skills are important and can be taught and courses are now more common in schools, in-company training, and even in prisons.

So far however, results have been mixed. What these courses definitely can achieve is a raised awareness of soft skills like empathy. This means that even if a manager lacks empathy, he or she can learn to be aware of its importance, understand the theory, and take pro-active steps to compensate for any weakness in this skill area.

Be careful!

1. In many places, the definition of **soft skills/hard skills** is simplified to mean *'people skills'* and *'academic skills'*
2. Be aware of the related terms **soft power** and **hard power**. This distinction is used in international diplomacy. The power a nation has in terms of cultural influence, leverage of global institutions, and membership of international alliances is sometimes described as **soft power** while **hard power** describes pure military and economic power (when economic power is used to impose punitive measures like sanctions).

10. Supply and Demand

Example:

What makes the price of petrol (gasoline) go up and down so much?

What does it mean?

The *law of supply and demand* is arguably the most important principle in free market economics.

Supply means the amount of a product that is produced by producers.

Demand means the amount of a product that is consumed by consumers.

The important part is how changes in **supply** and **demand** affect the **scarcity** (relative lack) and price of the product:

If supply drops and demand is unchanged, the price will increase (go up).
If supply increases and demand is unchanged, the price will decrease (go down).
If supply is unchanged and demand drops, the price will decrease.
If supply is unchanged and demand increases, the price will increase.

It works the same for services too: if there is only one hairdresser in town (supply shortage), he or she can charge a premium (high price) for haircuts, choosing the richest customers. With more competition (raised supply), the price of haircuts will probably go down. On the other hand, if the population of the town goes down (lowered demand) and there are too many hairdressers, the price may become so low that some hairdressers will probably close up. If the population increases (increased demand), then the price of a haircut will remain stable or even go up, encouraging even more hairdressers to open up shop.

How to answer:

Fluctuations in world - and local - oil and petrol prices are the result of numerous complex factors including war, politics, monopolies, subsidies, tax, investment, and development. The most basic and important factor however, is the law of **supply and demand**. *If for any reason supply falls, the price of oil will probably rise and vice-versa: any oversupply risks flooding the market and dramatically lowering prices. Conversely, any significant rise in demand - often caused by a sudden change in energy policy or a period of accelerated development - will also send prices skyward, while sluggish growth and a cautious economic outlook tend to have the opposite effect.*

Be careful!

This book offers a very simple definition of the law of supply and demand and this is more than you need for the C1 exam - the real-world intricacies of supply and demand can be fiendishly complicated but for the C1 exam you needn't worry about technical economic theory. Simply knowing what the words 'supply and demand' mean, is enough. In everyday English, people often say '*...well, it's about supply and demand...*' meaning: the price is not just about the quality of the product, or *'just because I'm the boss doesn't mean I get to choose my price'.*

UNIT 9 TEST!

Fill in the gaps using the keywords from this unit.

1. A local _____ has recently celebrated her first year in business after starting up the city's first bicycle delivery company.

2. I was thinking of taking out a loan to buy a new car until I saw how high the _____ was!

3. After being twice over-charged by my bank, I demanded to speak to the person _____ customer complaints.

4. On paper, the interview candidate had great qualifications but it soon turned out he lacked the _____ required for the job.

5. After my business failed five years ago I was left with a lot of _____, which I am still paying off now.

6. Following two years at the company, Alison wanted more challenge and responsibility and so she applied to her boss for a _____.

7. Andy, a supermarket worker, was awarded a prize for being _____ of the month.

8. David couldn't understand why houses were so expensive in the UK even though he accepted that it all came down to _____.

9. I spent a lot of money last month but fortunately my bank statement shows that I am still in _____.

10. I thought I was doing pretty well in my new job but the _____ I received from my boss in my first review was very critical.

11. With over 600 workers, the pie factory was the largest _____ in the town.

12. I'd like to buy a house but until I get a better job I don't think I'll be able to get a _____ from the bank.

13. Office _____ can usually be significantly improved with just a few simple re-arrangements of furniture and equipment, according to experts.

14. The government's new education policy is under review after encountering a number of problems during _____.
Opposition politicians have criticised the policy as badly thought-through and overcomplicated.

Answers: 1. *entrepreneur* 2. *interest* 3. *in charge of* 4. *soft skills* 5. *debt/debts* 6. *promotion* 7. *employee* 8. *supply and demand* 9. *credit* 10. *feedback* 11. *employer* 12. *mortgage* 13. *productivity* 14. *implementation*

Congratulations! You've completed 90% of your essential exam vocabulary revision for the C1 exam! You're nearly there!

UNIT 10: POPULAR CULTURE AND INTERNET

This is a tricky topic because it will almost certainly be included in the C1 exam, but it deals with new technology, new fashions, new attitudes and new words which may be considered 'non-standard' (until they become so everyday that they are considered 'standard English').

Furthermore, the new attitudes and fashions that examiners choose to feature in the exam will most probably reflect an 'anglo-centric' view of the world. Depending on your nationality and culture, these attitudes and fashions might seem either totally normal or a little strange.

It's because these words are a little bit special and also a favourite exam topic, that a selection is included here.

1. Crowdsourcing *and* Crowdfunding

Example:

How do you think recent internet-enabled developments like **crowdsourcing** *and* **crowdfunding** *have changed the way people do business?*

What does it mean?

'The crowd' is a general term for *'audience'* or simply *'the people'*. *'Outsourcing'* is a technical business term for paying people outside the company to complete tasks for the company.

Crowdsourcing means obtaining knowledge, skills, solutions, ideas or some other constructive input from either your target audience or 'the people' in general. This may be paid or unpaid, and usually facilitated via an internet-based platform.

The internet - and more specifically, online social networks in tandem with smartphone and wifi proliferation - has enabled entrepreneurs, companies, and non-profit organisations to communicate with large numbers of people more easily and (potentially) more effectively than ever before.

Wikipedia is a good example of a not-for-profit **crowdsourced** enterprise - the contributors who add content can be any individuals with a computer and an internet connection, splitting a mammoth task between hundreds of thousands or even millions of people.

On a more commercial level, film producers and fashion designers now routinely ask their followers for creative input, effectively **crowdsourcing** the basic ideas for the next big film or clothing trend.

Alternatively, crowdsourcing may simply refer to the practice of advertising or allocating one-off jobs - or *'gigs'* - online. This type of work is often referred to as *'the gig economy'*.

Crowdfunding means advertising a business plan or charitable cause online with the intention of collecting investment or donations from internet users.

How to answer:

*I think big companies have realised that **crowdsourcing** offers a way of developing a closer relationship with consumers, and online 'fanboy' forums provide businesses with a valuable resource for informed feedback and market research. The real story however, in my opinion, is the way **crowdsourcing** and **crowdfunding** have created a new generation of self-employed workers. On the positive side, young entrepreneurs no longer need to have the right connections or seek expensive loans from the bank in order to pursue an innovative new business idea. On the negative side, many self-employed workers in the so-called 'gig economy' work unsocial hours for low wages with no guaranteed work from day-to-day, and no paid holiday or sick leave.*

Be careful!

Be aware that not everyone agrees with which activities may or may not be called 'crowdsourcing' and 'crowdfunding'.

2. Download from/upload to/share on/share with

Example:

Is there any difference between file-sharing and video/music piracy?

What does it mean?

*To **download from** the internet is to save files that are made available via the internet.*
*To **upload to** the internet is to transfer files from a device to an internet server.*
*To **share on** the internet is to transfer files to a filesharing network or social media network or shared server.*
*To **share files with** someone means to transfer files from your private device to somebody else, or give somebody access to files on your private online space.*

How to answer:

If it concerns copyrighted media then the law is clear: **sharing on** *the internet is copying and you can be prosecuted, either for* **uploading** *copyrighted material* **to** *the internet, or for* **downloading** *copyrighted material* **from** *file-sharing sites. It is however, perfectly legal to* **share** *your self-created media, or open-source media* **on** *the internet or* **with** *your friends.*

Be careful:

1. You probably know these basic internet terms but for maximum points you should make sure you get the <u>prepositions</u> right! Prepositions are not vital for passing the C1 but getting them right is important in 'use of English' questions and also helps you to sound more fluent and polished.
2. Some people prefer to use 'upload **onto**'.

3. FOMO (fear of missing out) and YOLO (you only live once)

Example:

Are **FOMO** *(fear of missing out) and* **YOLO** *(you only live once) connected?*

What does it mean:

FOMO and **YOLO** are examples of acronyms (a phrase, name, or term that is shortened by taking the first letter of each word in the phrase) which have become popular via instant messaging chat and social media.

How to answer:

FOMO *(fear of missing out) and* **YOLO** *(you only live once) represent an attitude which has itself been partly caused by internet culture: an urgent desire to experience all things and all places (as seen on the internet) as quickly as possible. Even* *using acronyms suggests a need to save time and space. Clearly, FOMO and YOLO are two sides to the same coin: while YOLO is the confident mantra of the fun-seeker, FOMO expresses the anxiety caused by seeing that other people are having (or appear to be having) more fun than you are. With social networking sites swamping us with photos and videos of our friends' and celebrities' activities, it can feel like all this fun and excitement is happening somewhere else while you are sat at home alone, staring at a screen. It's important to remember that this media is curated - deliberately selected and polished - and does not reflect the full reality of a person's day. It's also important not to get trapped on the treadmill of instant gratification: cheap thrills and novelties are okay in themselves but long term, meaningful happiness and success usually requires long term thinking, personal goals, and commitment.*

Be careful!

Acronyms are generally considered non-standard English so should always be introduced with explanations in parentheses (like this).

4. Millennial

Example:

*Do you agree that **Millennials** tend to be entitled and lazy?*

What does it mean?

Until recently, **millennial** was simply the adjective form of '*millennium*', meaning a period of 1000 years. The word still has this meaning, but has also been used since the late nineties, with increasing frequency, as a noun-person to describe anybody reaching adulthood in the early 21st Century (or people with birth dates roughly between 1980 and 2000, also referred to as '*gen-Y*').

The term is based on the Strauss-Howe theory that people (in the USA) of a similar age are likely to share certain beliefs and behaviours that make them different from previous or later generational groups. Not everyone agrees with this theory - cultural background, social class, education, religion, and wealth are routinely put forward as being far more important than date of birth in determining beliefs and behaviour. However, the theory fits in neatly with the generally-accepted idea that history can be divided into static periods interrupted by periods of change. The idea of a 'generational group' is also backed up in raw numbers by the fact that (in the west) the millennials are the largest demographic group since the baby-boomer generation (born roughly 1940s - 1960s).

There is also much disagreement about exactly how old millennials are - with many people arguing that the group should be split in two to reflect the impact of the digital revolution from the mid-nineties on - and what behaviours set the 'digital natives' apart.

According to the media, older people tend to see millennials as entitled (i.e. they believe they have an automatic right to things) impatient for success, wasteful with money, and lazy in regard to commitment and hard work. Millennials are said to describe themselves as variously idealistic, ambitious, empathetic, uncertain, anxious about the world's problems, image conscious, and pressurised by debt, education, and social media.

How to answer:

I think on the outside, millennials can sometimes appear lazy and entitled - especially if they happen to be privileged and spoiled but I also think this is a huge generalisation and largely the result of older generations comparing what they see of today's youth to their own youthful experiences forty or fifty years ago - and the world has changed dramatically since then.

One of the big differences is that things like clothes, holidays and tech - which were much more expensive fifty years ago - have become much cheaper, while really important things like education and housing have become far more expensive compared to average salaries. So older people look at millennials spending money on fashion, holiday experiences and smartphones, and say 'this is why they can't afford to buy a home - I had a home when I was their age because I saved money and worked hard.' The truth is that homes are now so expensive and clothes so cheap that this argument doesn't make any sense. Millennials know that they have to study or work for low wages in insecure jobs for years before they have any chance of buying a house and getting that stability - clothing and smartphones don't make any real difference.

Be careful!

1. **Millennials** are NOT '~~people born in 2000~~' - millennials are people born between 1980 and 2000, reaching adulthood 'in or around the beginning of the new millennium'.

2. People born roughly between 1965 and 1980 are usually referred to as '*generation X*'

3. Millennials may also be referred to as '*generation Y*'

4. People born in the year 2000 or after are often referred to as '*generation Z*' and may also be referred to as '*digital natives*', having grown up from birth with digital technology. Later millennials (born between 1990 and 2000) may also be referred to as digital natives.

5. Profile

Example:

In what ways should your online business **profile** *differ from your online personal* **profile**?

What does it mean?

Profile literally means the shape or outline of something, usually as viewed from the side. Coins often feature the face of a monarch or leader 'in profile'.

Figuratively, **profile** and *outline* mean a summary of the most basic information about something, usually a person, a company, or a country.

On the Internet, a **profile** is the basic information or 'front page' of a social networking account, usually including a name, a 'profile picture' (a photo or logo) and maybe a brief description and some contact details. A **profile** is 'what people can see from the outside'.

How to answer?

Firstly, you need to consider the name you choose - personal profile names are often playful and informal and for most types of business such names are inappropriate. For a business profile you should use your formal title and name together with your profession, role, or position.

Secondly, your profile picture for a business profile should ideally be professionally-taken against a blank, neutral background and be rather conservative than informal - no holiday snaps or group photos! You don't need to wear formal business attire but something suited to your job is best.

The other big difference between your personal and business profiles is that you may not want your personal contact details to be made available publicly. By contrast, a business profile will usually provide some means of contact - even if it is only the general company email address or telephone number.

Be careful!

You probably know all about **online profiles**; be aware of the other meanings of **profile**!

1. The verb **to profile** means to make a general assessment based on first impressions. **Racial profiling** describes a form of prejudice, usually official, when assumptions are made about a person, based on ethnicity or skin colour.
2. A **company profile** may refer to a visual chart or graph showing the company's value and financial performance.
3. **Profile** may also be used generally to talk about a person's public image and level of exposure or fame. This use of the word is often used with 'high' and 'low' - **high-profile** means *famous, in the public eye, in the media*; **low-profile** means *discreet, incognito, kept out of the public eye* - often deliberately.

6. Progressive *and* Conservative

Example:

*Does Graham describe himself as **progressive** or **conservative?***

What does it mean?

Generally, **progressive** refers to politically left-leaning policies and supporters. Typical policies include **progressive taxation** (the higher your income the higher rate of tax you pay), equal rights for women and minorities, environmental protection, state-services (health, education, legal support).

Generally, **conservative** refers to politically right-leaning policies and supporters. Typical policies include tax breaks for higher earners and large corporations, traditional family values, and minimal government intervention in the free market.

Generally speaking, a **progressive attitude** is one which readily embraces social change, while a **conservative attitude** is one which is protective of tradition and cautious about social change.

How to answer:

*Graham describes himself as socially **progressive** in terms of equal rights for women and minorities but economically **conservative** in regards to tax policy and the welfare state.*

Be careful!

1. Politics is something that most teachers and examiners avoid - and yet it is an essential part of daily life and often the top issue in daily news. Increasingly, politics is discussed in the wider sphere of social media and lifestyle choices so there is always a chance some political vocabulary might find its way into the C1 exam. **Progressive** and **conservative** are two of the most basic political words so it's a good idea to be familiar with these words and the associated concepts.
2. In the United Kingdom, the words 'conservative' and 'conservatives' may also refer to '*the Conservative Party*' and its supporters. The Conservative Party and the Labour Party, are the two major political parties in UK politics.

7. Retro, classic, and classical

Example:

What kind of music do you prefer: funky **retro**, *rock and pop* **classics**, *or* **classical**?

What does it mean?

This trio of words is a good example of how meanings can be fluid and slippery - especially when it comes to fashion and popular culture!

Retro usually means a style or fashion associated with a previous decade, imitated or reinvented in the present time. The most typical retro fashion period is the late 1960s but the term has been applied to styles and fashions associated with every decade in the 20th Century - especially 'classic' styles and fashions which are bold and bright and instantly recognisable.

Classic is used in a general way as a positive term of approval for any style or fashion or work of art or music which is widely praised or makes a strong statement, and stands the test of time. In some languages, the word 'evergreen' is used to describe these songs, films, and fashion designs; in English, these are called classic songs, classic films, and classic designs. An example of a **classic rock song** is '*Smoke on the Water*' by Deep Purple, while Jacob Jacobsen's *L1* desk lamp is considered a **design classic**.

This should not be confused with **classical** which refers primarily to the Greek and Roman periods in European history and associated art and culture. Second to this, **classical** is also used to refer specifically to a period in European art and music (roughly 1750-1820) between the baroque and romantic periods and includes the works of Mozart and Beethoven. In art and architecture, the classical style takes inspiration from ancient Greek and Roman styles and emphasises regular form, clean lines, and mathematical proportions. Third, **classical music** is often used in a more general way to refer to a tradition of western 'art music' or 'serious music' from the middle ages to the present day.

How to answer:

I enjoy a bit of funky **retro** *at the right kind of party but at home I tend to listen rather to new bands and artists. I like the rock and pop* **classics** *but they get played too often. I sometimes listen to* **classical** *music but I prefer folk music.*

Be careful!

1. The word **retro** comes from the word '*retrograde*' which has the simple meaning '*backwards*'. However, '**retrograde**' is also used in a negative way to mean 'primitive' especially when describing people or practices seen to be reverting back towards the primitive and savage.

2. The word **classics**, as in '*the classics*' may be used interchangeably with '*classical studies*', the the academic subject concerned with ancient Greek and Roman culture, language, literature, and history.

8. Status

Example:

*Is a **status** update an effective substitute for an email?*

What does it mean?

From the word '*state*', **status** means 'the essential condition or form' of something. Often it means the level of progress or development. It is also used formally to describe whether someone or something is available or unavailable; active or inactive. **Relationship status** concerns whether someone is single, in a casual or serious relationship, or married.

In social media terms, the word **status**, used on its own, simply means 'what I am doing/feeling right now' and is used to describe a general post (comment or media) that is made available to a general friendship group or the general public.

How to answer:

I think this question makes the assumption that people nowadays send less emails and text messages because social media allows us to instantly communicate with almost everyone we know. Obviously this presents advantages and disadvantages: being able to communicate so easily means that we are able to keep in touch with more people than we probably would have before. On the negative side, the issue is probably quality. Whereas previously a person might have written a personal email to a close friend, nowadays it's easy to get lazy and just post a general **status** *update for your five hundred 'friends'. I would have to agree that* **status** *updates are effective in reaching large numbers of people quickly and easily but if you want to connect personally with someone you have to invest a bit more time and effort, and do so with more privacy and intimacy, too.*

Be careful!

'Static' and 'stationary' are different words that are used to describe something that is not moving or does not move. 'Static' may also refer to 'static electricity' or 'static interference' in radio transmission.

9. Trend, Trendy, *and* Trending

Example:

What is the current **trend** *in house prices, according to the article?*

Are **trendy** *mums and dads embarrassing?*

If a news story is **trending**, *does that make it important?*

What does it mean?

A **trend** can either be a new fashion or it can refer more generally to a consistent pattern or general movement in a certain direction, especially when describing statistical data.

Trendy is a synonym for 'fashionable'.

Trending refers specifically to any news story or point of interest which receives a lot of searches and comments online.

How to answer:

According to the article, the current **trend** *in house prices is upward: prices have risen again in the past quarter and are set to rise further, although the analyst predicts a gradual slowdown.*

Are **trendy** *mums and dads embarrassing? It depends on who you ask and what you mean by* '**trendy**'. *For many teenagers, parents are embarrassing whatever they do, but especially if they display themselves in public. On the whole, it's probably better if your parents pay attention to their appearance and stay interested in current styles and interests. However, if 'trendy' means middle-aged people dressing like teenagers this can be embarrassing for everyone, although there will always be some rock-star mums and dads who successfully carry it off.*

Trending *news items may concern serious, important events and issues but often they are trivial: celebrity gossip, a new toy, a joke or meme ...of course, these things can be said to be important in certain ways, even if only as a way of reflecting current times and interests, but this is clearly a different kind of importance to that associated with political decisions and global crises, which affect people's lives in serious and dramatic ways.*

Be careful!

Trending up and **trending down** are usually used in a financial context to talk about stocks and shares.

10. Viral

Example:

Suggest ways in which an educational writer can help his book **go viral** *on the internet.*

What does it mean?

Viral is the adjective form of '*virus*', referring to infections either biological or software based.

In the context of social media, **viral** is used figuratively - and usually in a positive way - to describe a media item which is shared very rapidly and soon spreads around a country or the world via the internet:

*What started off as a joke between a few friends soon became a **viral video** sensation.*

How to answer:

*Despite millions of people studying and practising things like e-marketing and social media management, the magic formula behind **viral** internet hits remains a holy grail, a philosopher's stone. Standard practice involves using various platforms and media formats but perhaps the very nature of internet novelty means that even if there is a formula, it is always changing.*

Educational books are an unlikely source of global sensation but they do provide the promise of concrete and measurable results - as long as the purchaser actually reads the book!

Be careful!

Don't confuse the adjective **viral** (rapidly shared) with a computer virus (malicious code designed to corrupt files or disable computer operation).

UNIT 10 TEST!

Fill in the gaps using the keywords from this unit.

1. 'Fear of missing out', known popularly as _____ can be seen as the negative side of the 'you only live once' mantra, also known as _____.

2. After getting a new job in a prestigious law firm, Jacqueline was advised to modify her online _____ as it was too informal.

3. Although she was born in 1996, Lena didn't like being called a _____.

4. Always on social media, Robert updated his _____ several times daily.

5. Catherine downloaded an app which alerted her to the _____ news stories of each day.

6. Gabriella successfully raised the money needed to start her business by using a _____ platform on the internet.

7. Gibbon's History of the Decline and Fall of the Roman Empire is a _____ work of historical investigation and analysis that set the standard not just for _____ studies but for historical writing in general.

8. Jake believed in old-fashioned values and traditions and was accordingly resistant to anything that sounded too _____.

9. Once Peter had completed his CV, he _____ it to a special networking site for professionals.

10. The video footage of the baby and the cat singing together went _____ overnight, with nearly a billion shares worldwide.

Congratulations! You've completed 100% of your essential exam vocabulary revision for the C1 exam!

Hopefully you already feel more confident and prepared.

If you have also completed your general preparation, including exam task practice, and you are scoring 70% or more, you are ready to take the C1 test!

If you have time, try practising the exercises in this book again, and also use the wordlist on the next page to check any words you are still unsure of.

Good luck with your exam!

WORD LIST
(BY UNIT)

(1) Tasks and analysis I

Aspects
Contradict
Convey
Discuss
Factors
Infer
Influence
Outweigh
Perspective
To what extent

(2) Tasks and analysis II

According to
Address *and* Tackle (a problem or issue)
Distinguished (from)
Emphasise
Features
Illustrate
Innate
Outcome
Significance *and* Relevance
Summarise

(3) B2 level mistakes

Be used to
Delicious
For example
Fun *and* Funny
In common (with)
Look forward (to)
Until
Sympathetic
Whether
Work *and* Workplace

(4) Connectors

Accordingly
For this reason
Furthermore
In the same way
In other words
One example of this is
So what I mean is
Surprisingly however
Ultimately, it comes down to
Which brings me to

(5) Phrasal verbs and idioms

Get the gist
Get to the heart of (sth)
Play down
Relate to *and* identify with
Set the tone
Take (sb/sth) for granted
Take (sth) well/badly/to heart
Tend to/Tend towards/Be prone to
Try to work out how
Zero in on (sth)

(6) Discursive language

Assume
Associate (with)
Attribute to
Concerned with *and* Concerning
Considering that *and* Compared to
Determine
Exaggerate
Given (that)
Stress (sth)
Support (an opinion, claim, or theory)

(7) Functional speech verbs

Advise
Admit *and* Deny
Argue
Caution (against)
Claim
Counter
Conclude
Concur
Speculate
State

(8) Feelings (Verb-3 adjectives)

Amused
Challenged
Daunted
Exhilarated
Enlightened
Inspired
Intrigued
Misled
Overwhelmed
Threatened

(9) Business and finance

Credit, debt, interest, *and* mortgages
Employee *and* Employer
Entrepreneur
Feedback
Implementation
(to be) In charge (of something)
Productivity
Promotion
Soft skills *and* Hard skills
Supply and Demand

(10) Popular culture and internet

Crowdsourcing *and* Crowdfunding
Download from/upload to/share on/share with
FOMO (fear of missing out) and YOLO (you only live once)
Millennial
Profile
Progressive *and* Conservative
Retro, classic, and classical
Status
Trend, Trendy, *and* Trending
Viral

ABOUT THE AUTHOR

Albert Bowkett studied English and American Literature at Manchester University in the UK and spent several years working in children's services before training to be a teacher of English as a foreign language in 2010. Since then Albert has helped hundreds of students and professionals from a range of different countries and backgrounds to develop advanced level English and achieve their goals.

This is his second book, following the publication of *C1 speaking Skills: Simple Tools for Advanced English.*

Printed in Great Britain
by Amazon